Series / Number 01-047

The Grievances of Military Coup-Makers

WILLIAM R. THOMPSON
Florida State University

 SAGE PUBLICATIONS / Beverly Hills / London

For information address:

SAGE PUBLICATIONS, INC.
275 South Beverly Drive
Beverly Hills, California 90212

SAGE PUBLICATIONS LTD
St George's House / 44 Hatton Garden
London EC1N 8ER

International Standard Book Number 73-8 7846

Library of Congress Catalog Card No. 0-8039-0309-X

FIRST PRINTING

When citing a professional paper, please use the proper form. Remember to cite the
correct Sage Professional Paper series title and include the paper number. One of the
two following formats can be adapted (depending on the style manual used):

(1) NAMENWIRTH, J. Z. and LASSWELL, H. D. (1970) "The Changing Language of
American Values." Sage Professional Papers in Comparative Politics, 1, 01-001.
Beverly Hills and London: Sage Pubns.

OR

(2) Namenwirth, J. Zvi and Lasswell, Harold D. 1970. *The Changing Language of
American Values.* Sage Professional Papers in Comparative Politics, vol. 1, series no.
01-001. Beverly Hills and London: Sage Publications.

CONTENTS

The Grievances of
Military Coup-Makers

WILLIAM R. THOMPSON
Florida State University

In the numerous attempts to explain the occurrences of military coups, analysts have employed a variety of approaches and themes that roughly can be clustered into four categories:

(1) the "pull" of regime vulnerability

(2) the "push" of the military subsystem

(3) the "push and the pull" of the world system and its various subsystems

(4) the "push-comes-to-shove" of coup-maker grievances.[1]

Explanations of regime vulnerability generally revolve around an image of the military being pulled into direct political action by weaknesses in the regime and in regime leadership and/or by socioeconomic and political underdevelopment. Those who espouse the second approach choose to stress the basic resource superiority and organizational characteristics of the military establishment (relative to the regime) that tend to push the military organization into direct political action. Advocates of the third approach point out the implications and consequences of systemic interdependencies at various levels of political interaction, the possibility of "coup contagion," and the pervasive activities of transnational and penetrating actors. The fourth approach takes the view that coup-making is a risky enterprise and therefore it is reasonable to assume that the individual coup-makers have motives, grievances, and goals of their own for which they are willing to assume the risks of death, imprisonment, exile, or demotion. While analysts tend to emphasize one approach at the expense of the others, there is no pressing reason to view the four approaches as mutually exclusive. Each approach is capable of improving our understanding of military coup behavior. Presumably, a synthesis of the four would provide a full explanation. Regrettably, such a synthesis would be somewhat premature in the absence of still further cultivation within each of the four vineyards. In particular, the fourth approach—coup-maker grievances—rarely has left the bailiwick of political historians and journalists. In part, this problem can be traced to the dominant style of analyzing political violence. Stone (1966: 164) has pointed out that,

> Everyone is agreed in making a sharp distinction between long-run underlying causes—the preconditions, . . . and immediate, incidental factors—the precipitants, which trigger the outbreak and which may be nonrecurrent, personal, and fortuitous.

The debatable implication of this distinction is that social scientists safely can ignore the "triggers" and not risk omitting "anything that matters from a practical standpoint" (see Eckstein, 1965: 140-141). To the contrary, an underlying thesis of this paper is that pre-coup events and processes are dismissed too readily as unique, ephemeral, and unmanageable factors. The grievances of the military coup-makers are very likely necessary (although rarely sufficient) as preconditions to the event. To dismiss or to ignore them is to seriously distort what military coups are about. Consequently, this paper will concentrate solely on an empirical inventory of military coup-maker grievances. Several questions will be of central concern. What are these grievances? Are they uniform throughout the world and constant over time? Are they all of equal importance in bringing about military coups? The answers provided by this paper will not be exhaustive on the subject. Hopefully, however, the answers will contribute to improving our understanding of military coups as well as stimulating greater interest in the systematic analysis of those grievances that help bring about human conflict.

DATA COLLECTION AND CODING PROCEDURES

The reason for collecting and for analyzing grievance data is to shed some systematic light on why military coups (here defined as the removal or the attempted removal of a state's chief executive by the regular armed forces through the use or the threat of force)[2] occur in the most proximate sense—from the perspective of those individuals and groups apparently responsible for planning and executing the coups. Ideally, one might endeavor to interview a random sample of the large and scattered population of relevant subjects. However, even if time and money were available for such an heroic task, the receptiveness and usefulness of the available interviewees is dubious. Presumably, the next best course would be what historians and area specialists do in the field: they ask local informants—both participants and spectators of the events in question— and they study previous descriptions of the events, all toward the goal of reconstructing what transpired in order to infer why it might have taken place. However, this project proposed to study all the military coups between 1946 and 1970.[3] Regardless of its legitimacy, the traditional approach simply will not suffice for an analytical universe that encompasses 25 years and 274 military coups in 59 states[4] (see Table 1). An alternative course would be to make use of those who have already taken the traditionally favored route to produce their versions of political history. Relying on these accounts, it was possible to piece together a number of grievance outlines for each military coup. While information is

TABLE 1
A SUMMARY OF MILITARY-COUP FREQUENCY (1946-1970)

Coup Frequency	Number of States	States
1	17	Cambodia, Costa Rica, Equatorial Guinea, Ethiopia, Gabon, Iran, Jordan, Lebanon, Libya, Mali, Nepal, Nicaragua, Oman, Senegal, South Yemen, Uganda, Upper Volta
2	9	Burma, Central African Republic, Egypt, France, Ghana, Greece, Somalia, South Korea, Togo
3	7	Burundi, Zaire, Cuba, Pakistan, Portugal, Sierra Leone, Turkey
4	3	Colombia, El Salvador, Nigeria
5	6	Algeria, Congo (Brazzaville), Dahomey, Indonesia, Panama, Yemen
6	2	Dominican Republic, Honduras
7	2	Haiti, Sudan
8	2	Paraguay, Thailand
9	5	Brazil, Guatemala, Laos, Peru, South Vietnam
11	1	Iraq
12	1	Ecuador
14	1	Syria
16	1	Argentina
18	2	Bolivia, Venezuela

probably not complete for any single case, the data base appears to be sufficient to warrant the largely descriptive exploration presented in this paper.

SOURCES

The sources utilized were not exhaustive but still quite extensive. One hundred and seventy-one political histories and country/case studies of varying length and eight world and regional news digests (see Appendix B) provided most of the information for this study. Each of the eight news digests was consulted for every relevant coup. This turned out to be worthwhile not only for the variety of information obtained but it also helped to ensure that few cases would go undetected.[5] The political histories and the indexes of the New York *Times* and the *Times* (London) also were used for the initial coup search. When the other sources failed to provide sufficient grievance material, the appropriate newspaper accounts were consulted as a last resort.[6] On the average, two political histories, one world news summary, "one-half" regional news summary, and "one-half" newspaper article were consulted for each coup. These figures refer only to those sources that actually yielded data.[7] The availability and quality of information was anything but uniform. This is reflected in Table 2, which provides a regional breakdown of the average number of sources utilized by source type as well as by Appendix C, which provides the same information for each country. Most Arab coups are covered fairly well by political histories, while the best sources for African coups proved to be the various news digests. The figures in Table 2 for Latin America are deceptive. A few states such as Brazil, Argentina, and Colombia are well covered by all types of sources but especially by political histories. Other

TABLE 2
AVERAGE NUMBER OF SOURCES UTILIZED PER COUP FOR ACTUAL DATA-MAKING PURPOSES

	Source Types			
	PH	WD	RD	NA
World	1.89	.98	.47	.56
Latin America	1.46	.85	.52	.74
Arab	3.12	1.04	.35	.43
S.E. and E. Asia	2.06	1.17	.00	.42
Sub-Sah. Africa	1.58	1.18	1.08	.34

NOTES: PH = political histories and country/case studies; WD = world news digest; RD = regional news digest; NA = newspaper article.

states such as Paraguay and Panama, and consequently their coups, virtually have been ignored. With some exception, Asian coups proved to be the most difficult in terms of information acquisition.[8] Understandably perhaps, the lion's share of contemporary attention has been focused on other facets of Asian politics. While it would be difficult to fault this study for a lack of sources, it must be acknowledged that the very multiplicity of sources creates problems of "adequacy." Data for different parts of the world must be obtained from different types of sources, and ironically, the less information available on a military coup, the greater the reliance on the least reliable of the four source types—the newspaper account. Still, it would appear that these problems only can be resolved by a more equal interest in some of the more "remote" parts of the globe. In the interim, data-making is restricted to sources that are currently available. This project attempted to utilize as many as were considered feasible.[9]

CODING CATEGORIES AND PROCEDURES

In order to partially control for this analyst's own preconceptions about coup-maker grievances, the coding categories were determined only after an open-ended collection of the reputed motivations for each coup was assembled.[10] Once these had been examined, a coding scheme was devised and imposed upon the heretofore unstandardized information (see Figure 1).

	Corporate	Not-So-Corporate	Societal Residual
Sources and Objects of Conflict	Position and resource scarcities and standings	Position and resource scarcities and standings	Position and resource scarcities and standings
Grievance Level	The military organization	Elites factions sectional groups	Society
Discussion Topics	Protection and advancement of organizational positions and resources	Protection and advancement of sub-organizational positions and resources	Political ideology Social reform Order maintenance
		Personnel adjustments	

Figure 1: AN ANALYTICAL SCHEME FOR MILITARY COUP-MAKER GRIEVANCES

The specific grievances display a variety of motivations ranging literally from the petty to the profound. Nevertheless, they do exhibit several discernible dimensions that render them susceptible to generalized inquiry. Mack and Snyder (1957: 218) in a now dated but still unrivalled review of conflict behavior research have summarized that literature by stating that conflicts arise from position and resource scarcities. Position scarcities occur in situations where actors cannot occupy the same roles or perform similar functions simultaneously. Resource scarcities arise when the supply of desired objects or states of affairs is restricted to the extent that actors cannot have all that they desire of whatever values they seek. The military coup, a form of conflict behavior, is essentially a small-scale internal war fought over positions and resources. But the question remains: whose positions and resources? The answer to this empirical question provides a basic handle for categorizing military coup-maker grievances. Corporate grievances encompass those conflicts that stem from the fact that military coup-makers are socialized members of a more or less professionalized organization with interests and needs of its "own." Hence, corporate grievances are concerned with the position and resource standing of the military organization. But within the military organization, there are elites, factions, and minority groups each with their own positions and resource standings to protect and to advance. Thus, a second category—not-so-corporate grievances—refers to conflicts that are sometimes linked to corporate loyalties and perceived interests but which more acutely reflect the elementary behavior of elites and suborganizational groups engaged in political competition. Finally, military coup-makers occasionally are concerned with the societal distribution of positions and resources. They may seek to preserve or to alter the prevailing distribution. Or they may choose to require other actors to attempt their alterations in an orderly manner. This creates a need for a third category, labeled the "societal residual," for in fact, few coups tend to fall into this cell. Appendix A lists the coding subcategories and their definitions.

Temporarily united in diverse coalitions, military coup-makers usually can be expected to have multiple and sometimes conflicting motives. Coups were coded for multiple grievances as dictated by the sources consulted.[11] And since the same sources rarely indicated the relative salience of each grievance in any systematic fashion, no attempt was made to distinguish between motives said to be more or less important. Furthermore, since grievance packages are multifaceted, none of the three major categories is mutually exclusive, nor are all of the subcategories nonoverlapping. Vis-à-vis the major categories, "personal adjustments" provides a good example. The five types of adjustment are nonoverlapping and are considered to fall under the major category of not-so-corporate grievances. Yet some of the types, particularly "preemptions," may have both corporate and societal overtones. A different sort of example is provided by the six subcategories of corporate positional grievances. The six were coded separately only to facilitate a closer examination of the positional grievances that seem to matter to the military coup-makers. They easily might have been collapsed into one subcategory, but with a subsequential and unnecessary loss of information. In short, the reader should not infer that military coups are either corporate, not-so-corporate, or societal in terms of their grievance foci. Or that coup-makers concerned with corporate autonomy may not also be concerned with military pay shortcomings or coalition-reductionist threats. Grievance packages simply do not work that way. Nevertheless, the main purpose of this paper is to provide a descriptive breakdown of the various types of grievances that may or may not be merged by any particular coup-making group. In the process, the various elements of grievance packages will be discussed as if they were divisible components and not as the multidimensional and tangled wholes actually experienced in the politics of the military coup d'état.

Finally, it must be fully acknowledged that alleged or reputed motivations are certainly not the same thing as actual motivations. The data base is nowhere near as hard as one optimally would prefer and it is clearly at the mercy of the quality and the comprehensiveness of past scholarly and journalistic reporting. Considering the nature of the approach, it is quite possible that any particular type of grievance will have been proportionately under or overrepresented. And the resulting analysis can be considered no less tentative than any other study characterized by soft data, crude methods, and a largely gross cross-national perspective. [12] Still, social science and its practitioners have learned to accommodate themselves to what they can obtain until they are in a position to do better. As long as the reader keeps in mind the various imperfections of the data collection and analysis, no misunderstandings need occur over what this paper represents—an attempt to provide a generalized and proximate approach to explaining military coups. It is hoped that those students who are dismayed by the partial perspective on coup behavior that emerges in this paper will take it upon themselves to improve the data base. Only in this fashion will our understanding of the politics of the military coup progress.

CORPORATE GRIEVANCES

Organizations, and military ones are no exceptions, are perceived by their members to have certain "needs" that must be fulfilled if the organization is to remain a going concern. The needs of military organizations include autonomy, hierarchical discipline, functional monopoly, security, prestige, honor, and an adequate level of supply inputs (i.e., men, equipment, training, and financial and policy support). These needs are scarce social goods that make it necessary for the military to compete with other organizations and groups for its share of a limited pie. Conventionally, components of a government's coercive apparatus, regular armed forces must direct their main competitive efforts at the government's nominally controlling leadership—the regime incumbents. Thus the fulfillment of military needs becomes primarily but not exclusively a contest between the regime and the military's leadership and one in which to a unique degree the military is able to personify its own well-being with that of the nation-state. To further compound the situation, military organizations tend to establish ecological niches within their various socio-eco-political systems. These niches represent behavioral spaces that function as bounded territories embellished with myth and tradition and requiring protection and defense from external infringements. Failure to respect these boundaries, deliberate or otherwise, is perceived as a threat to the military organization's "turf" or territorial imperative.

POSITIONAL GRIEVANCES

Military coups are, in part, the consequences of perceived failures on the part of the regime in satisfying or respecting the military's needs. Six extremely intertwined positional needs are identifiable among the host of attributed coup motivations: (1) autonomy, (2) hierarchy, (3) monopoly, (4) cohesion, (5) honor, and (6) political position. The numbers reported in Table 3 suggest that these corporate positional factors, considered in isolation, are not the most significant of coup-maker grievances. Yet they need only be considered in isolation for purposes of elaboration; for they do not arise in isolation but as integral parts of larger and more complex grievance packages. As such, they constitute an important beginning to dissecting the military coup.

Autonomy

Military coup-makers apparently perceive a threat to the military's scope of independent control over its general organizational activities.

TABLE 3
CORPORATE POSITIONAL GRIEVANCES (CPG)
(in percentages)

		1946-1950	1951-1955	1956-1960	1961-1965	1966-1970	Total
World	(n's)	(32)	(25)	(55)	(65)	(52)	(229)
Any CPG		(32)	36	11	25	25	23
Autonomy		6	16	4	9	8	8
Hierarchy		0	12	0	5	8	4
Monopoly		3	20	0	9	10	7
Cohesion		0	0	2	9	4	4
Honor		6	12	6	5	4	6
Political Position		16	16	4	12	6	10
Latin America	(n's)	(23)	(17)	(29)	(22)	(10	(101)
Any CPG		17	35	10	36	20	23
Autonomy		4	12	3	9	0	6
Hierarchy		0	12	0	9	20	6
Monopoly		4	29	0	9	0	8
Cohesion		0	0	0	23	10	6
Honor		0	12	7	9	0	6
Political Position		13	12	3	18	0	10
Arab	(n's)	(4)	(5)	(7)	(16)	(14)	(46)
Any CPG		75	60	0	25	14	26
Autonomy		25	40	0	13	7	13
Hierarchy		0	20	0	6	0	4
Monopoly		0	0	0	19	7	9
Cohesion		0	0	0	0	0	0
Honor		50	20	0	6	0	9
Political Position		25	40	0	19	7	15
S.E. and E. Asia	(n's)	(4)	(2)	(12)	(13)	(3)	(34)
Any CPG		25	0	8	15	33	15
Autonomy		0	0	0	15	0	6
Hierarchy		0	0	0	0	0	0
Monopoly		0	0	0	0	0	0
Cohesion		0	0	0	0	0	0
Honor		0	0	8	0	0	3
Political Position		25	0	0	8	33	9
Sub-Sah. Africa	(n's)	(0)	(0)	(2)	(10)	(22)	(34)
Any CPG		0	0	50	20	27	26
Autonomy		0	0	0	0	14	9
Hierarchy		0	0	0	0	14	9
Monopoly		0	0	0	10	18	15
Cohesion		0	0	50	10	0	6
Honor		0	0	0	0	9	6
Political Position		0	0	0	0	5	3

From the military perspective, corporate autonomy refers to what Gutteridge (1970: 21) has coined aptly "martial freedom," that is, the number and the nature of activities the regime allows the military to do for themselves. Therefore, the regime's degree of control over the military and the military's degree of autonomy are inversely related. This need not be a zero-sum situation, but may become one should the military's zone of acceptance for regime control fall short of the regime's need to establish and expand its sphere of influence over its own coercive apparatus. Conflict may arise when the regime attempts to expand the boundaries of its control zone at the expense of the military establishment or vice-versa. This threat of infringement is all the greater to the extent that the military desire near-absolute self-government. As Wesson (1967: 482) has observed, military organizations have throughout time expressed a "mentality of separateness," and devised their own rules and values as well as socioeconomic systems in the process of segregating themselves from a civilian world. The boundaries of this sometime near-total subsystem are extremely sensitive and regimes are advised to violate them only at their own risk. An outstanding example of a civilian regime's encroachments on corporate military autonomy is the case of pre-1966 Ghana.[13] As part of a larger attempt to improve his political control, Nkrumah cracked down on the armed forces. Military aid sources were diversified against professional advice. Separate military units were created and maintained outside the official command structure. It was made quite clear that the military were to be used domestically in a manner to which they were disinclined by training. Toward this end, personnel were required to undergo ideological indoctrination. Abrupt changes were made in the senior command structure; career advancement became especially politicized. Combined with other grievances, the Ghanaian officer corps had become ripe for a military coup. While Welch (1970: 34-35) does not appear to be correct in suggesting that the desire to protect professional autonomy "is perhaps the most widespread and potent motive for intervention," his observation may well be close to the mark in terms of potency.

The next four factors are intricately related to corporate autonomy and in fact are salient and overlapping elements in maintaining the corporate parameters of military life.

Hierarchy

Military coup-makers apparently perceive a threat to the military's organizational chain of command.

Hierarchical discipline, the backbone of the military's authority system, is an important means of maintaining organizational self-control. Disrupting hierarchical stability is a threat to the military leadership's continued capacity for both self-control and organizational effectiveness. An example is offered by the Brazilian coup in 1964. Less than a week before the coup, President Goulart had refused to punish the sailor participants in a pro-Goulart strike/mutiny. The Navy minister resigned in protest. Goulart also had been lenient in handling an attempted N.C.O. coup the year before. Rowe (1964) states that it was believed widely that Goulart was planning or encouraging acts of military insubordination to advance his own political plans. While these factors were not the sole cause of the 1964 coup, they cannot be dismissed as trivial, for they apparently were not ignored by the coup participants.

Monopoly

Military coup-makers apparently perceive a threat to the military's functional claim to existence as the nation-state's principal, legitimate organization of armed force.

Functional monopoly is an important component of the corporate self-image qua mission and therefore a significant aspect of its raison d'être. Since rival military or paramilitary forces usually are created by regimes that desire a counterbalance to the power of the regular armed forces, there is always the very real possibility that the irregular forces could entirely displace the military both in terms of function and organizational existence. In addition to the lack of professional military control over them, the rival forces also divert scarce resources. A passive military may even find itself "out-gunned" by a better armed party militia or police force. Therefore, miltary coups that serve to suppress or to disband rivals, particularly in Sub-Saharan Africa, where this threat has been twice as common as elsewhere, can be viewed as expressions of perceived organizational self-defense.

Cohesion

Military coup-makers apparently perceive a threat to the military's organizational unity.

The significance of organizational cohesion is greatly similar to that of hierarchical discipline. Perceived attempts to render military organizations less cohesive or united are seen as threats to the stability of its authority system as well as continued organizational effectiveness (see Skidmore,

1967: 121-122). A fairly recent example is the 1966 coup in Argentina. While the coup was primarily one of a long series of anti-Peronist actions, a faction of the coup coalition, the "Frontists," were believed not to be particularly anti-Peron but acted rather to prevent a threat of "impending internal conflict" within the armed forces (see Springer, 1968: 163). In fact, one of the immediate precipitants of the coup had been President Illia's dismissal of the army commander-in-chief for his attempt to arrest another army general who supported Illia's conciliatory policies toward the Peronistas.

Honor

Military coup-makers apparently perceive a threat to the military's collective self-esteem.

Military honor and prestige are essential ingredients of the military ethos. Pride in organizational membership is crucial to consolidating individual loyalties to the corporate body. Not unlike the medical profession and for similar reasons, the military profession has enveloped itself with a mystique of service to the community. In return for this altruistic service, the military feels entitled to a noble and honorable social image. To impugn the military's sense of honor and prestige is then an attack on the members' self-esteem and identity as members of the corporate military group. Such instances of "psychological violence" (see Strickland, et al., 1968: 46) have arisen when civilian legislatures have laid the blame for defeat in war at the doorstep of the army, as occurred in Syria prior to its first coup in 1949. This "stab-in-the-back" syndrome may be a form of collective psychological compensation according to Finer (1962: 61). Less directly, the problem also may arise where officers feel that a regime's incompetence has made the nation—and thus its standard bearer, the military—a standing joke to the outside world. Afrifa (1966: 113), a coup-maker, expresses feelings along this line in his book, *The Ghana Coup.*

Political Position

Military coup-makers apparently perceive a threat to the military's organizational relationship with the political system.

This last factor is not, at first glance, a universal attribute of military organizations. Actually, the defense of an organization's position in the political system is best viewed as lying on a continuum. Where the armed forces have established themselves as powerful political interests represents one extreme; where the armed forces prefer as little direct political participation as possible would demarcate the opposite extreme (an "apolitical" position). Both extreme positions as well as the less clear in-between points require defense. Odd as it may seem, civilian attacks on an "apolitical" preference can bring about a military coup. The two November 1955 Brazilian coups have been called "anti-coup" coups in that their apparent purpose was to prevent a military faction, the *golpistas,* from seizing control and nullifying the October election victory of the Kubitschek-Goulart ticket. The coups were executed by the "legalists" under the banner that the will of the electorate must prevail. The inauguration of Kubitschek and Goulart took place on schedule thanks to the two military coups. More common, however, is the defense of an entrenched, corporate-dominant political position. In early 1951, a Syrian civilian regime attempted to remove control of the gendarmerie from the ministry of defense. Without the police, the government recognized that it would possess no enforcement capability independent of the army. The army, on the other hand, desired to retain control of the gendarmerie to better ensure its own electoral control.[14] A military coup resolved the issue in favor of the army. With the exception of Sub-Saharan Africa, the defense of a well-established military position in the political system appears to be the most common of the six corporate positional factors. Given time, African armies also will create positions that require defense. After all, the "needs" of autonomy and monopoly required relatively little time to develop south of the Sahara.

RESOURCE CONFLICTS

Positional conflicts are generally intermingled with another type of corporate grievance—the conflict over resources. These can be divided into four subtypes: (1) dissatisfaction over pay, promotions, appointments, assignments, and/or retirement policies; (2) dissatisfaction over budget allocations, training facilities-policies, and/or interservice favoritism; (3) dissatisfaction over general military policy and/or support for military operations (i.e., war, insurgency, and the maintenance of order); and (4) some combination of the first three subtypes. As indicated in Table 3, one out of three military coups involves one or some combination of resource grievances. The ratio is much higher in Arab and Asian coups. The reasons for the relatively low proportional presence of this factor in Latin America will become more apparent in the not-so-corporate section of this paper. Interestingly, the world summaries demonstrate one of the few clearly ascending trends, although the potency of the measures may have reached a proportional ceiling in the last decade. The trend also indicates that this type of corporate conflict has more than doubled as a prevalent motivation of military coups during the 25-year period. Considering the interregional distribution of corporate factors in both Tables 3 and 4, Nordlinger (1970: 1138) would appear to lack support for his hypothesis that one cannot expect corporate military values to be as strong in areas where the armed forces are of recent creation and lack a history of tradition and extensive socialization. The newest armed forces are to be found in Africa and Asia. Yet, military coups in these regions seem no less motivated by corporate grievances, with the exception of several positional factors in the case of Asian coups, than elsewhere.

Type A

Military coup-makers are apparently dissatisfied with the state of one or more of the following concerns: pay, promotions, appointments, assignments, and/or retirements.

Military pay grievances are as old as armies. Symbolically, salaries reflect in part the organization's worth to the regime and to society. Rarely do the symbols match the soldier's expectations and image of self-worth. The problem is exacerbated if exposure to European and North American salary scales sets artifically high standards of remuneration for poor and weak regimes to emulate (see Lee, 1969: 92). This has been said to be an important factor in Sub-Saharan Africa, where regimes have been especially prone to austerity budgets yet have dared not reduce military salaries (Bell, 1965: 8). More materialistically, income is a determining factor for the individual's ability to control his immediate environment. Officers on fixed governmental salaries are extremely vulnerable to economic inflation. The same can be said of civilian bureaucrats, but the military have more "persuasive" means of rectifying their financial plights, at least in the short run.

Promotions, assignments, and retirement policies are particularly prone to becoming politicized by regimes that seek ways to ensure military loyalties. Officers loyal to the current regime may receive the quickest promotions and key assignments. Those of dubious allegiance are apt to be assigned to remote areas, given desk jobs to remove them from effective control of troops, or retired early. There is always an intraorganizational political element in these policies, no matter what political roles the military assumes. But when these policies do become especially politicized by regime leaders, two consequences are evident. The less political and more professional personnel are aggravated by policies favoring incompe-

TABLE 4
CORPORATE RESOURCE GRIEVANCES (in percentages)

Type		1946-1950	1951-1955	1956-1960	1961-1965	1966-1970	Total
World	(n's)	(32)	(25)	(55)	(65)	(52)	(229)
A		6	24	15	15	17	15
B		3	0	4	3	2	3
C		0	0	13	12	12	9
D		6	4	2	8	8	6
Total		15	28	34	38	39	33
Latin America	(n's)	(23)	(17)	(29)	(22)	(10)	(101)
A		4	29	10	14	10	13
B		4	0	7	5	0	4
C		0	0	0	0	0	0
D		0	0	0	0	10	1
Total		8	29	17	19	20	18
Arab	(n's)	(4)	(5)	(7)	(16)	(14)	(46)
A		25	20	14	19	14	17
B		0	0	0	0	0	0
C		0	0	14	13	29	15
D		25	20	0	19	7	13
Total		50	40	28	51	50	45
S.E. and E. Asia	(n's)	(4)	(2)	(12)	(13)	(3)	(34)
A		0	0	17	23	0	15
B		0	0	0	0	0	0
C		0	0	42	23	67	29
D		0	0	8	8	0	6
Total		0	0	67	54	67	50
Sub-Sah. Africa	(n's)	(0)	(0)	(2)	(10)	(22)	(34)
A		0	0	50	10	18	18
B		0	0	0	10	5	6
C		0	0	0	10	0	3
D		0	0	0	10	5	6
Total		0	0	50	40	28	33

NOTES: A = dissatisfaction over pay, promotions, assignments, and/or retirement policies. B = dissatisfaction over budget allocations, training policies, and/or interservice favoritims. C = dissatisfaction over general military policies and/or the level of support for military operations (e.g., war, insurgency, and order maintenance). D = some combinations of A, B, and/or C. Consequently, if a subfactor is followed by six columns of "0", it is not necessarily totally absent unless subfactor D also is followed by six columns of "0."

tent and unqualified but loyalist officers, while those most directly affected by the personnel policies may realize that they must remove the incumbents before their own political control capabilities are seriously weakened. Either group or both in coalition may resort to the coup in order to eliminate a very direct threat to their career possibilities. These factors figured prominently in the events preceding the 1952 Egyptian coup despite that coup's reputation for being the epitome of the thrust of modernization and reform. A successful coup, of course, does not guarantee that these career irritations and threats will be removed along with an incumbent. The second Ghanaian coup (1967), for example, was executed by junior officers who resented the promotions assumed by the 1966 coup leadership and their own dismal promotion future (see First, 1970: 398).

Type B

Military coup-makers are apparently dissatisfied with the state of one or more of the following concerns: budget allocations, training arrangements, and/or interservice favoritism.

It seems surprising that an element that many people would suspect to be of prime importance to military coups—the matter of defense allocations—proves to be a very minor factor. Only six coups apparently involved this issue or one related to it. Since this is surprising, an examination of different data is particularly warranted. Ignoring the outcome of Table 4, one might expect some relationship between the years in which defense budgets declined and the years in which military coups occurred. Table 5 reports the results of such an examination.[15] Five columns are listed. The first column, "total years," summarizes the proportional distribution of years in which relative defense budgets increased, decreased, or did not change. The second column gives the corresponding proportional distribution of years in which military coups occurred and in which budgets increased, decreased, or did not change. If military coups are associated with budget declines, one would look for a larger proportion of "military-coup years" (second column) in the budget decrease row than would be anticipated by knowing the total configuration of fluctuations (first column). Table 5 indicates that years in which military coups occurred were more likely to coincide with years in which relative defense expenditures increased, not decreased.

The third column gives the appropriate distributions for the years immediately prior to "military coup years" and provides a $(t-1)$ lag with which to test the relationship. While pre-coup years tend to coincide

slightly with the lack of budget fluctuations, again, no coup-budget-decline association is disclosed. Finally, columns four and five examine the first (t+1) and second (t+2) years after "military coup years."[16] This information is useful in two respects. One, it is possible that the defense expenditure data may be based upon budgetary projections. One would then be forced to wait a year or two for any coup-budget-decrease relationship to appear. Two, and partially in contradiction to the first point, an examination of the post-coup years may show whether budget increases follow coups. With one exception, the decrease proportions of columns four and five are not noticeably different from the standard set by the first column. The exception is the 12% difference between columns one and five, evidenced for successful Arab coups. The problem of interpretation then becomes one of whether we are dealing with projections or actual budgets in year one. Considering the other two rows in the same column, it is readily evident that relative defense expenditures in the Arab world are likely to change two years after a successful coup, but they show an equal tendency to change in either direction. So, if we are dealing with projections, one cannot way that military coups are most likely to coincide with budget declines in the Arab world. More generally, it would appear that there is a tendency for relative defense expenditures to rise in the years after a coup, especially after successful coups. However, this tendency does not necessarily undermine the reported outcome for corporate resource conflicts—type B. It may simply mean that post-coup ruling arrangements are more likely than their predecessors to augment the status of military allocations. A causal link to coup-maker motivations cannot be assumed.

As for the apparent, general lack of association between coups and defense budgets, three caveats deserve to be mentioned. First, the examination was restricted to a quite limited n. Only the budget fluctuations of those states that have experienced coups were considered and serial data were available for only half of the relevant n. While one conceivably would expect any association to be strongest in areas where coups are experienced, more complete data and more sophisticated measurement techniques might yield different results. Second, relative defense budgets do not appear to be subject to wide fluctuations. In some parts of the world, defense budgets are a "given" of political life and consequently may not require violent protection. Third, and related to the second qualification, there is always the good possibility that a threat to severely reduce defense spending would provoke remedial action prior to any actual reduction. This situation would not be revealed necessarily by the data used to produce Table 5. However, it should be reflected in the grievance data and was not.

If it can be accepted that coup grievances are not closely linked with defense spending levels or fluctuations,[17] the possibility still remains that coups are connected to the arms trade or to the more specific nature of defense spending. The argument is a familiar one. Where the military is politically important, the demand for arms is likely to be satisfied. Satisfying the demand for arms helps to ensure that the military remains politically important. Despite the evident logic of this indirect linkage contention, the most extensive study of the third-world arms trade yet to appear (SIPRI, 1971: 41-59) fails to establish any direct link between military coups and the demand for arms. Using the SIPRI data, it is possible to make a further test of the argument that military coups are associated with fluctuations in the supply of arms and/or consequently contribute to the demand for arms.

The SIPRI data is ordinal and therefore extremely awkward to deal with in terms of annual flux. They quantify the annual flows by the scores: 1 = less than $10 million; 2 = $10–$50 million; 3 = $50–$100 million; and 4 = more than $100 million. Consequently, an annual decrease from "3" to "2" or no change (two successive scores of "3," for example, could involve variable changes as high as $50 million!) makes for only a rather crude attempt to evaluate these fluctuations. In fact, the insensitivity of this examination may be reflected in the large proportions of "no change" reported in Table 6.

The examination reported in Table 6 was conducted in the same manner as discussed in relation to Table 5. Most of the same caveats also apply. With several erratic exceptions, Table 6 shows few conceivably significant intercolumn percentage differences. Comparing the first two columns, there is some evidence for a relationship between "military coup years" and declines in weapons flows for Asia and Africa. The percentage differences range from 5-10%. If there is a relationship, it may well be for different reasons. Asian armed forces have been embroiled in various protracted conflicts with weapons needs approached only by the appetites of the Arab-Israeli and Indo-Pakistani conflicts. Whereas, African armies are the newest and the smallest and may feel a need to "catch up" quickly with the rest of the world. As for the notion that military coups in turn contribute to the world's arms trade, it appears to be slightly supported by post-coup-year flow increases in all areas (particularly in Latin America) save, surprisingly, Sub-Saharan Africa. It is possible tentatively to conclude that while the demand for arms is generally not a significant factor (noting the two regional exceptions) in precipitating military coups, there does appear to be a slight aggregate tendency for armed forces to augment their weapons stocks in post-coup periods. At the same time, it is difficult to

TABLE 6

FLUCTUATIONS IN THE FLOW OF MAJOR WEAPONS AND
"MILITARY COUP YEARS" 1950-1969 (in percentages)

Weapons Fluctuations	Total Years	Coup Years	Pre-Coup Years	Post-Coup Years (1)	Post-Coup Years (2)
All Coups					
"All" (n=46)					
Increase	21	22	19	26	23
Decrease	19	22	19	23	22
No Change	60	56	62	51	55
Latin America (n=14)					
Increase	18	20	19	29	24
Decrease	20	20	20	24	22
No change	62	60	61	47	54
Arab (n=9)					
Increase	26	34	27	30	32
Decrease	22	19	23	33	32
No change	52	47	50	37	36
S.E. and E. Asia (n=7)					
Increase	21	26	17	28	16
Decrease	17	26	17	22	10
No change	63	48	66	50	74
Sub-Sah. Africa (n=14)					
Increase	20	12	12	14	19
Decrease	18	28	16	14	24
No change	62	60	72	72	54
Successful Coups					
"All" (n=40)					
Increace	20	23	21	26	21
Decrease	21	20	18	21	26
No change	59	57	61	53	53
Latin America (n=14)					
Increase	18	21	17	33	29
Decrease	20	15	20	20	23
No change	62	64	63	47	48
Arab (n=7)					
Increase	29	35	44	33	29
Decrease	24	12	25	27	42
No change	47	53	31	40	29
S.E. and E. Asia (n=7)					
Increase	21	27	18	18	29
Decrease	16	36	18	27	42
No change	63	36	64	55	29
Sub-Sah. Africa (n=10)					
Increase	20	18	6	14	8
Decrease	18	23	13	14	25
No change	62	59	81	71	67

NOTES TO TABLE 6
NOTES: Major weapons include aircraft, naval vessels, armored fighting vehicles, and missiles; states included are: Algeria, Argentina, Bolivia, Brazil, Burma, Cambodia, Central African Republic, Eolombia, Congo (B), Cuba, Dahomey, Dominican Republic, Ecuador, Egypt, El Salvador, Ethiopia, Gabon, Ghana, Guatemala, Haiti, Honduras, Indonesia, Iran, Iraq, Jordan, Laos, Lebanon, Libya, Mali, Nigeria, Pakistan, Paraguay, Peru, Senegal, Somalia, South Korea, South Vietnam, Sudan, Syria, Thailand, Togo, Uganda, Upper Volta, Venezuela, Yemen, and Zaire.
SOURCE: SIPRI, 1971: 404-688.

segregate the connection between coups and the arms trade from the connection between coups and other forms of warfare, both internal and external. Prime examples would be the Yemeni and Nigerian civil wars, which were precipitated by military coups and which certainly affected the demand for arms. The continued presence of regional rivalries equally tends to confuse any attempt to establish a direct causal connection between the arms trade and military coups.

Type C

Military coup-makers are apparently dissatisfied with the state of one or more of the following concerns: general military policy and/or the level and nature of support for military operations (e.g., war, insurgency suppression, and order maintenance).

Conflicts of this sort largely arise in two circumstances. The first is during or in the aftermath of a defeat at war. The first Syrian coup was a complicated affair, but among its motivational components was the issue of blame for the defeat in the first Arab-Israeli war. Civilian politicians blamed the military for the loss. The military considered a number of civilian politicians responsible. Both sides were prepared to penalize the other side for the loss. A military coup enabled the military to act first and more decisively. The coup was made all the easier by the particular vulnerability of a regime that had headed an unsuccessful war effort (see Khadduri, 1953: 520; Rustow, 1963: 10-11; Andreski, 1961: 60). Several later coups in Iraq, Egypt, and Syria also have involved similar issues of war defeat.[18] The second situation arises in states experiencing insurgencies. What happens is that a difference of opinion on the method of suppression often develops between regime leaders and the military commanders. In the 1965 case of the Congo (now Zaire), President Kasavubu proposed a reconciliation with insurgent leaders and with the African states that had assisted in the rebellions. Mobutu, the army chief of staff, violently disagreed with these proposals and also feared that Kasavubu intended to replace mercenaries with Ghanaian troops. As usual, other factors were operating, but the dispute over insurgency operations shortly was resolved by a military coup (see Willame, 1970: 142-143).

NOT-SO-CORPORATE GRIEVANCES

There is a great deal more to the military coup than corporate factors alone. The personnel engaged in coup activity have personal, factional, and sectional interests to pursue as well. With these suborganizational pursuits, however, the analytical distinction between positions and resources becomes more blurred. Particularly at the personal level, positions often become another type of resource. Consequently, the discussion of not-so-corporate grievances will not attempt to maintain overtly the basic distinction employed in the previous section of this paper. Implicitly, though, the sources and objects of conflict remain the same in the abstract sense. The grievance foci merely have shifted.

INDIVIDUAL

Military coup-makers apparently perceive a threat to their personal position(s) and resource base(s) either within the military organization, the political system, or both.

A category focusing on individual interests can be extremely misleading. It usually can be assumed that every military coup's leadership obtains some form of personal gratification in seizing control of the state. Coup-makers may see themselves as national saviors, popular liberators, or the guardians of cherished order and tradition. They may desire status, popularity, wealth, power, or more generally, the means for enhancing control of their personal environment via control of the public environment. Several writers have in fact placed particular stress on these less-than-noble motivations in explaining military coups (see Kling, 1962: 137-138; Andreski, 1968: 208-209; Lee, 1969: 176-179). Unmistakable examples are not too difficult to find. One Bolivian general, Antonio Seleme, had been a leader of a 1951 coup that denied the presidency to the M.N.R. candidate. A year later, he was prepared to offer his services to neutralize part of the army and to provide police support to an M.N.R. conspiracy. He argued that his inclusion in the coup coalition would improve the chances of success from 60 to 80%. All he asked for in return was the Bolivian presidency. The M.N.R. leadership agreed (see Brill, 1967: 12). The 1952 effort eventually was successful, but Seleme deserted at an early stage in the fighting when success seemed unlikely.

This study takes for granted individual venality and subconscious motivations that can be found in all spheres of political activity. To say that a particular coup leader craves political power very well may be true, but such an explanation does not suffice in differentiating the military coup-maker from the "normal" politician seeking election in a country that has never experienced a military coup. Nor is politics, even in the coup zone, quite the Hobbesian jungle of constant competition for spoils and prizes one might expect if events were to be understood primarily in terms of avarice, lust for power, and survival of the fittest. Rather, the personal interests summarized in Table 7 refer to specific pre-coup events and regime actions that are apparently interpreted by the coup leaders as personal threats to their own political resources and positions. Classical examples abound. Prior to the first Syrian coup, a scandal had developed over responsibility forproviding the army during the first Palestinian war with inferior cooking oil. The civilian regime was prepared to arrest the army officer who supervised food supplies. Hearing of the impending arrest, the army chief-of-staff hid the suspected officer either for reasons of personal friendship, corporate loyalty, or fear of personal implication. The first Syrian military coup (1949) came immediately after civilian investigators had discovered the hiding place, and was led by none other than the army chief-of-staff (see Seale, 1965: 42-43). In mid-1953, the Colombian army uncovered a plot to assassinate its commander, General Rojas Pinilla. When the army refused to release one of the plot's conspirators, President Gomez ordered Rojas Pinilla's resignation. The next day, a military coup led by Rojas Pinilla instead removed Gomez (see

TABLE 7
INDIVIDUAL INTERESTS (in percentages)

	1946-1950	1951-1955	1956-1960	1961-1965	1966-1970	Total
World						
(n's)	(32)	(25)	(55)	(65)	(52)	(229)
%	34	28	33	32	35	33
Latin America						
(n's)	(23)	(17)	(29)	(22)	(10)	(101)
%	39	29	17	32	50	31
Arab						
(n's)	(4)	(5)	(7)	(16)	(14)	(46)
%	25	40	71	38	29	39
S.E. and E. Asia						
(n's)	(4)	(2)	(12)	(13)	(3)	(34)
%	0	0	42	31	33	29
Sub-Sah. Africa						
(n's)	(0)	(0)	(2)	(10)	(22)	(34)
%	0	0	50	20	32	29

Fluharty, 1957: 137-139; Galbraith, 1966: 153). An Indonesian intra-army conflict in which the chief-of-staff, General Nasution, was attempting to consolidate his position through army reorganization and the transfer of certain officers culminated in three attempted military coups in favor of Colonel Zulkifli Lubis, whose army and political position was most threatened by Nasution's plans (see Feith, 1962: 504-506). In 1966, a popular officer in the army of the Congo (Brazzaville), Captain Marien Ngouabi, was demoted and about to be transferred to the political hinterlands. Protest demonstrations by Ngouabi's tribesmen were joined by army personnel who forced the detention of government officials in the capital's sports arena. Since the army was not united, a compromise eventually was reached that included the rescinding of Ngouabi's demotion and transfer (see Africa Diary, 1966: 2963-2964; Keesing's Contemporary Archives, 1968: 22633-22634). As it turned out, the regime had reason for fearing Ngouabi; he later led two more coups, the second of which was finally successful (1968). It would be advantageous to recount a number of similar coup stories for, in terms of flavor, they probably reveal more about why coups occur than any statistical table or theory is capable of doing. The above four, however, must suffice for the category of the protection and advancement of personal political resources and positions. Too many other categorical situations remain to be discussed.

SUBORGANIZATIONAL GROUPS

Military Factions

Military coup-makers apparently perceive a threat to the position(s) and resource base(s) of a suborganizational clique to which they belong.

Coup leaders occasionally are also the leaders or representatives of military factions—that is, cliques or parties within the military establishment. Guenther Roth (1968: 201) has stated that army leaders tend to become personal rulers once they are in power. Actually the tendency toward post-coup personal and patrimonial rule is often well established before the coup. Military organizations, not unlike other bureaucratic agencies, are prone to internal "patron-client" subsets. Some officers, distinguished by advanced position, professional distinctions, political connections, ideology, personal charisma, or some combination, attract the personal loyalties of other officers and their subordinates. Where the armed forces are less directly involved in politics, these patron-client factions are important to the intramilitary political system and career advancement. In military organizations more directly involved in politics, suborganizational cliques have the same function but intraorganizational rivalries become more intense. Political threats directed at a member of a faction either from within or without the military are perceived as threats to the entire faction. Frequently, this is a correct perception. Military coups may be felt as necessary to prevent the ascendancy of a rival faction within the military, as was the case in Argentina in 1962. The Argentinian army, with a tradition of secret lodges, was split between *Azules* and *Colorados.* The question was not simply one of control of the military establishment but also one of control of the political state, for one virtually meant the other. Thus the "blues" and the "reds," differentiated by a host of factors: urban-rural backgrounds, colonial descent, occupational specialities, political ideologies, orientations to the military's roles in politics and the proper role of the Peronistas, fought a number of war games for real in the early 1960s initially over key command assignments but the struggles spiralled quickly to control of the political system.[19] One of the more ironic highlights of these 1962 conflicts was provided by the civilian president, who in the midst of one coup switched sides, thereby rendering the "loyalists" the "rebels" and vice-versa. The off and on polarization of the Argentinian army is an extreme example of the relationship of military factions to the military coup. As indicated in Table 8, military factions are even more prominent in Asian and Arab coups than in those of Latin America. Personal cliques appear to be particularly significant in Thailand, where many of the coups have focused on personalities to the virtual exclusion of genuine issues and ideological questions (see Wilson, 1964: 56). A large proportion of the Laotian coups involved in some way or another General Phoumi Nosavan, who had begun the contemporary coup cycle in 1959, and whose supporters were still attempting abortive coups six years later. The names of Nguyen Khanh, Nguyen Cao Ky, Pham Ngoc Thao, and Nguyen Van Thieu, some of which are only too familiar to American audiences, similarly and continuously reappear in a number of South Vietnam's recent coup leadership groups.

Sectional Groups

Military coup-maker(s) apparently perceive a threat to the position(s) and resource base(s) of a primordial or ethnoregional group to which they belong.

Just as military factions primarily are based on the cement of personal loyalties, the problem of primordial loyalties—loyalties based on primary groups distinguished by race, language, religion, tribe, family, and region—arises in the military coup. These sectional groupings also may

TABLE 8
MILITARY FACTIONAL AND SECTIONAL INTERESTS
(in percentages)

		1946-1950	1951-1955	1956-1960	1961-1965	1966-1970	Total
World	(n's)	(32)	(25)	(55)	(65)	(52)	(229)
Military Faction		13	24	31	32	17	25
Sectional Group		6	0	0	2	6	3
Both		0	4	4	8	17	7
Total		19	28	35	42	40	35
Latin America	(n's)	(23)	(17)	(29)	(22)	(10)	(101)
Military Faction		0	12	24	27	20	17
Sectional Group		4	0	0	0	0	1
Both		0	0	0	0	0	0
Total		4	12	24	27	20	18
Arab	(n's)	(4)	(5)	(7)	(16)	(14)	(46)
Military Faction		0	40	43	31	29	30
Sectional Group		25	0	0	6	0	4
Both		0	20	0	13	29	15
Total		25	60	43	50	58	49
S.E. and E. Asia	(n's)	(4)	(2)	(12)	(13)	(3)	(34)
Military Faction		100	100	50	69	0	62
Sectional Group		0	0	0	0	0	0
Both		0	0	17	15	0	12
Total		100	100	67	84	0	74
Sub-Sah. Africa		(0)	(0)	(2)	(10)	(22)	(34)
Military Faction		0	0	0	0	9	6
Sectional Group		0	0	0	0	14	9
Both		0	0	0	10	23	18
Total		0	0	0	10	46	33

overlap with military factions. Such cases frequently stem from colonial recruiting imbalances, which favored minority groups considered "more martial." With independence, states inherited armies in which strategic positions were filled by personnel of national minority status. These common primordial bonds enhance the cohesiveness of military factions, particularly in Sub-Saharan Africa and the Arab Middle East. Syria provides some of the best examples of coups involving ethnoregional antagonisms. Druze officers have been consistent adherents to coup coalitions especially in times of regime-Druze conflict. More recently, Syria has experienced a contest between two formerly allied minorities, the Alawi and the Druze, over control of the military and hence the state.

In Africa, similar contests, not always so clear-cut, between Ibo and Hausa (Nigeria), Tutsi and Hutu (Burundi), Fon-Fulani (Dahomey), to name a few, have surfaced in recent military coups.[20] As powerful as military socialization patterns can be, they are never so complete as to erase totally allegiances held prior to and during military service nor can institutional loyalties totally override personal allegiances made in the process of military service. The military coup can be an expression of corporate collective orientations, but it is just as or even more likely to be a reflection of smaller collectivities not representative of the military whole. Suborganizational groups, whether they be military factions, ethnic minorities, or both, also have access to the military coup to protect and to advance their resource and positional interests.

Elements of the armed forces also may seek and are sought for alliances with small opposition parties or the disgruntled wings of a ruling party. Most of the alliances indicated in Table 9 have been made with the same few parties. More than half of the Arab cases have involved the Ba'th, a party which could never muster sufficient electoral support in Syria or Iraq. A third of the Latin American cases represent Bolivian military elements allied with either the Socialist Falange or the M.N.R. and its factions. In all these cases, it is never completely clear who is using whom.

TABLE 9
ALLIANCES WITH OPPOSITION OR RULING PARTY FACTIONS
(in percentages)

	1946-1950	1951-1955	1956-1960	1961-1965	1966-1970	Total
World						
(n's)	(43)	(34)	(61)	(77)	(59)	(274)
%	23	12	16	18	9	16
Latin America						
(n's)	(32)	(26)	(35)	(31)	(12)	(136)
%	25	12	20	13	0	16
Arab						
(n's)	(4)	(5)	(7)	(17)	(16)	(49)
%	25	20	14	53	31	35
S.E. and E. Asia						
(n's)	(5)	(2)	(12)	(14)	(3)	(36)
%	20	0	17	0	0	10
Sub-Sah. Africa						
(n's)	(0)	(0)	(2)	(11)	(25)	(38)
%	0	0	0	9	0	3

It probably is not clear to the participants either. The previously mentioned Seleme case is illustrative of the ambiguity. Frequently, the military allies have different reasons for attempting to overthrow a regime than do their civilian partners and hence the coup coalitions are very much marriages of convenience.[21] In general, civilian parties are much more likely to be the victims of military coups rather than the beneficiaries. The few parties that do gain power through a coup alliance eventually become dominated by their military partners either in the name of the party or in the name of the military.

THE ADJUSTMENTS OF PERSONNEL

Military coups are particularly good examples of wars fought over the occupancy of political positions. Naturally, the removal of regime incumbents is definitionally intrinsic to the coup, but there is structurally more to these personnel wars than simply a negative focus on regime incumbents. Five personnel adjustment processes are discernible in military coups: (1) reductionist, (2) preventive, (3) preservative, (4) restorative, and (5) preemptive (see Table 10).

Reductionist

Military coup-makers apparently are attempting to reduce the size of a previously successful coup coalition or to anticipate or to counter the possibility of a reductionist effort.

The first process is most common in Arab and Asian military coups. The reductionist coup occurs in situations of post-coup attempts at reducing the size of a previously victorious coup coalition. Coup groups are not comprised necessarily of homogeneous political bedfellows. This is demonstrated by the variety of goals and grievances involved in any single coup. What is essential is that a number of coup entrepreneurs agree for whatever reasons that the time has come to remove a regime incumbent. Once this is accomplished, the conspirators agree to cooperate in order to achieve this minimally mutual goal. The most serious problems arise after success, when it becomes readily apparent that the initial coalition cement has dissolved or become weakened with the attainment of the initial objective. Then, the intracoalitional struggle for control may become most acute. Individuals and factions that earlier felt the need for the support of other individuals and factions no longer feel the necessity for this support and its attendant costs in terms of furthering their own goals.[22] Hence, the process of post-coup coalition reduction may bring about further

coups. An aspirant to primary post-coup control may seek to eliminate his coalition partners via additional coups or the partners may respond to such a threat by staging their own coup first. Recent political history in Algeria supplies the pluperfect illustration of the coalition reduction process and its consequences. Algeria became independent in 1962 in the midst of a civil war over the future leadership positions. The burden of the fighting for Algerian independence had fallen largely on irregular troops organized under provincial or *wilaya* commands. A more professionalized and better equipped army was forced by French border security to remain outside of Algeria until 1962. In June, the provisional government dismissed the leadership of the army's general staff in hopes of weakening the GPRA's political opposition. The professional army, headed by Boumedienne, teamed with Ben Bella, a civilian politician, and a few *wilaya* commanders to oppose the provisional government and its *wilaya* support's bid for control. The Ben Bella-Boumedienne coalition won the contest and Ben Bella assumed the new state's regime leadership. While a number of the *wilaya* commands were merged with the regular army, the positions of their former leaders were precarious. In 1963, Colonel Mohammed ou al-Hadj, fearing his removal from his command, revolted. A compromise was eventually reached as a result of the outbreak of the war with Morocco. In 1964, another former *wilaya* commander, Colonel Moham-med Chaabani, was relieved from his command in a regime attempt to further reduce the winning coalition. Chaabani also revolted but unsuccess-fully. During this time, Ben Bella had been attempting to strengthen his position vis-à-vis his primary coalition partner, Boumedienne. Toward this end, Ben Bella had attempted to divide the army by creating a popular militia headed by still another former *wilaya* commander, Colonel Tahar Zbiri, who was also promoted to army chief-of-staff. Ben Bella also attempted reconciliations with various opposition groups in order to prepare the way for new political alliances. Furthermore, Ben Bella began to remove Boumedienne's factional associates from the cabinet as early as 1964. Boumedienne, realizing what these actions amounted to in terms of his own political position, removed Ben Bella in 1965 before Ben Bella did the same to him. Boumedienne had managed to swing Zbiri to his 1965 coup coalition, but by 1967, Zbiri and other *wilaya* leaders realized that they in turn had been gradually removed from the regime's decision-making center. In November, Zbiri was ousted from his position as army chief-of-staff. Other *wilaya* personnel were removed from the F.L.N. party leadership. Consequently, Zbiri mounted an unsuccessful revolt in mid-December.[23] Thus, in each of the five revolts (1962, 1963, 1964, 1965, and 1967), one segment of a winning coalition had threatened the position of another segment, leading to a defensive coup response by the threatened.

A second type of coalition-reduction process involves coup "swingmen" (see Needler, 1968: 67-72). The need for swingmen arises in situations where the military is not united in its opposition to the regime, which does, in fact, seem to be the usual case. Needler has made the highly plausible observation that coup conspiracy originators are those most opposed to the regime incumbents. They are therefore at point E in Figure 2. There are some exceptions to this generalization depending on the type of coup, but in most cases Needler's observation is pertinent. The problem for coup-makers is that the officer corps will contain individuals along the hypothetical line between points A and E. The objective is to reduce the likelihood of significant opposition to a coup. This requires shifting officer orientations away from points A and B and toward points C, D, and E. One of the techniques for achieving this regime/coup orientation shift is to persuade certain individuals who have considerable prestige within the military, country, and/or world system to join the coup coalition thereby lessening the probability of opposition from any of the three quarters. The motives of these late adherents vary, but if the coup is successful they must usually be given a prominent position in the post-coup ruling arrangement. If they are not content to continue to serve as window-dressing for the coalition core, they must be removed if possible and if necessary by another coup. Egypt's Nagib is a well-known example of a cosmetic swingman who was eventually removed not without difficulty. The extended survival of Spain's Franco represents an unusual case of a swingman who managed to replace the core conspirators.

In general then, the coalition-reduction process comes into play when a

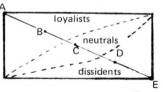

The most contented and most likely to defend the regime

loyalists

neutrals

dissidents

The most discontented and most likely to attack the regime

*Adapted from Gurr (1970: 276)

Figure 2: THE DISTRIBUTION OF MILITARY DISCONTENT*

heterogeneous coup group experiences intragroup conflict over who within the group will dominate after a successful coup. The process may result in further coups as early as two weeks after the original coup (Iraq, 1968) or as late as several years as in the cases of Egypt and Algeria.

Preventive

Military coup-makers apparently are attempting to forestall a perceived, extralegal attempt to prolong the stay in office of a chief executive.

Preservative

Military coup-makers apparently are attempting to assist an extralegal attempt to prolong the stay in office of a chief executive.

Restorative

Military coup-makers apparently are attempting to re-seat a chief executive deposed by a previous coup.

These three types of personnel adjustment processes are the least numerically important of the five. Preventive and preservative coups are those entailing respectively an attempt either to forestall or to prolong the regime incumbent's stay in office. In Latin America, this is referred to as the issue of executive *continuismo*. Whether originally popularly elected or installed in the aftermath of a coup, a regime leader may attempt to prolong his tenure through executive or legislative fiat or rigged elections as in Paraguay (1948), El Salvador (1948), and Honduras (1956). Military elements may oppose such an attempt at *continuismo* in order to safeguard constitutional processes or simply to assure the scheduled removal of an incumbent who is no longer considered desirable by the coup-makers and to forestall the possible consequences of his remaining in office beyond the time period he was originally allotted. Even more rarely, an executive fails to rig an election or plebescite successfully and must resort to a coup to ensure his bid for extended tenure as did Venezuela's Perez Jiminez in 1952. Alternatively, restorative coups attempt to re-seat an incumbent previously deposed by a coup. Again, such attempts may be motivated by desires to correct the illegality of the earlier deposition or simply to re-install a leader who was previously found to be more amenable or acceptable than the current incumbent. Perhaps significantly, restorative coups have become increasingly less frequent over the 25-year period and predominantly were unsuccessful. The most widely known case was the complicated 1965 civil war in the Dominican Republic which led to American and OAS intervention.

Preemptive

Military coup-makers apparently are attempting to veto the coming to power (whether legally or illegally) of a specific individual or group (whether civilian or military).

Of the five personnel adjustment processes, preemption numerically is the most common and is particularly characteristic of Latin American military coups. The process of preemption can be defined as an attempt to prevent an individual or group from securing or augmenting his or its degree of political control. Huntington (1968: 223-224) has called this type of coup the "veto intervention." Preemptive coups may occur in order to anticipate an imminent bid for control by another group of coup-makers. But the most likely situation is the electoral victory or imminent victory of a political party that is considered a threat to the military, both collectively and individually. This is a primary motivation for many military coups that precede or follow electoral decisions. In his study of successful Latin American coups (1907-1966), Fossum (1967: 235) found that 38% took place either six months before or after an election. Fossum's method of determining election years, however, was rather crude. He assumed that elections occurred on the average every six years and derived his percentage figure from this assumption. In the 1946-1970 period, coups were not quite so commonly associated with elections. Rather than assume the frequency of elections, each coup was coded positively or negatively for motivations reputedly connected to electoral decisions, before or after the fact. It is interesting to note that the proportional distribution of preemptive processes seems to be perfectly correlated with regional propensities to indulge in elections. Thus, if elections become more common in non-Latin-American areas, it is quite possible that more preemptive coups could be expected in the future (see Table 11).

The preemptive coup usually has strong corporate overtones. Radical parties, particularly Communist ones, are perceived or at least portrayed as direct threats to military institutions. This has been very much the case in Latin America ever since the Cuban army was reconstituted after Castro's accession to power. This is demonstrated graphically in Needler's thorough study of the 1963 Ecuadorian coup. Needler (1964: 41) had anticipated that strong anti-Communist orientations within the Ecuadorian officer corps were the result of: (1) class-based opposition to a Communist

TABLE 11
MILITARY COUPS AND ELECTORAL DECISIONS

		1946-1950	1951-1955	1956-1960	1961-1965	1966-1970	Total
World	(n's)	(43)	(34)	(61)	(77)	(59)	(274)
Preelection		7	9	15	12	7	10
Postelection		2	12	10	7	7	8
Total		9	21	25	19	14	18
Latin America	(n's)	(32)	(26)	(35)	(31)	(12)	(136)
Preelection		9	12	20	23	17	16
Postelection		3	12	14	10	8	10
Total		12	24	34	33	25	26
Arab	(n's)	(4)	(5)	(7)	(17)	(16)	(49)
Preelection		0	0	0	6	0	2
Postelection		0	20	0	12	0	6
Total		0	0	8	0	0	3
S.E. and E. Asia	(n's)	(5)	(2)	(12)	(14)	(3)	(36)
Preelection		0	0	8	0	0	3
Postelection		0	0	0	0	0	0
Total		0	0	8	0	0	3
Sub-Sah. Africa	(n's)	(0)	(0)	(2)	(11)	(25)	(38)
Preelection		0	0	0	9	4	5
Postelection		0	0	0	0	12	8
Total		0	0	0	9	16	13

economic program, or (2) religious opposition to Communism as astheistic, or (3) a functional opposition to violent domestic disorders associated with Communist movements. Instead, he found that the military was most likely to fear that the army would be disbanded and replaced by a militia if Communists should assume power. Even the hint of radical political influence appears to be sufficient to provoke this fear. A strong dyadic antagonism between a popular party and the military also may develop from a domestic variant of the "stab-in-the-back" syndrome. In 1948, the Indonesian army was in the process of resisting a Dutch blockade and other pressures. Simultaneously, the Communist party in East Java revolted and shortly was crushed by the army. Brackman (1969: 26-27) suggests that the army never forgot this incident. The 1948 army chief-of-staff in Java later became the armed forces chief-of-staff who presided over the purge of the Indonesian Communist party in 1965-1966. Similarly, in 1932, members of the Peruvian APRA captured a small army garrison during a revolt and liquidated the entire detachment. The

Peruvian army has both commemorated their deaths each year since and maintained a strong hostility toward APRA's political participation despite the mellowing of the party over the years (see North, 1966: 48-49).

Equally important is a not-so-corporate, self-perpetuating aspect. Needler (1968: 73) has pointed out that once a party's electoral victory is nullified or prevented by coup-makers, the coup group will have reason to believe that their own positions will be seriously jeopardized if the party should ever successfully assume political control. Thus, a political system can become subject to repeated preemptive coups as in Argentina where the position of the military institution and its leadership was maintained for some time at the expense of supporters of Juan Peron.[24] As Stepan (1971: 222-225) has observed, in the cases of post-Peron Argentina and post-1964 Brazil, the only way to avoid the hostility of the preempted is to stay in power.

SOCIETAL RESIDUALS: IDEOLOGY, REFORM, AND ORDER MAINTENANCE

DIFFERENCES OF POLITICAL IDEOLOGY

So far this paper has been remarkably mute on the role of political ideology. There is a reason for this reticence. But first, a note of clarification is in order. Military personnel have sets of beliefs pertaining to the various components of their environment. That there are corporate grievances indicates that the coup-makers have conceptions about what is proper for organizational welfare and regime-military relations. By the use of the phrase "political ideology," however, this section is concerned with that portion of coup-maker belief systems that relates to what is proper for society. In this sense, nearly 60% of the 274 coups examined could not be placed on even a very simple ideological spectrum. A possible reason is the inability of any single analyst to grasp totally the complex nuances and inflections of political beliefs around the globe. One example is offered by Jose Moreno's (1967: 164) analysis of the 1965 Dominican Republic spectrum in which he specified 12 positions on a continuum between extreme right and extreme left. The attempt, nonetheless, was made to code each coup group as being on the whole either more "liberal" or more "conservative" than the target of the coup. This is naturally a very subjective undertaking. The coding was guided in spirit by a delightful statement by Karl Menninger (1963: 86).

When certain individuals in society are comfortable under a certain political regime, any proposed change is apt to be seen as a threat. The proposers of such a change are called radicals. If some members of the comfortable society are not quite as comfortable as others and see some possible benefits in some change, they are called liberals. Both they and the stable group regard themselves as conservatives. But the radicals, on the other hand, who very much desire some kind of change, because it may benefit many, including themselves, regard those who oppose it as more than conservative, as reactionary against proposed progress."

"Conservatives" are thus more comfortable with the status quo than the "liberals." No attempt was made to make ideological classifications in the absolute sense. Each coup group was evaluated in comparison to the coup target. For this reason, "political ideology" is not advanced so much as a separate grievance category, but rather as an extra dimension or flavor that grievance packages may or may not possess. Of the entire coup population, 45 (16%) were judged to have had no apparent ideological character, at east in terms of differentiating the coup-makers from the chief executive. Twenty-nine (11%) coups were of a mixed nature. The coup coalition encompassed individuals and groups who were both more liberal and more conservative than the target. The opposing tendencies do not necessarily cancel each other out, but generally ideological divergences are restrained until the temporary coalition has served its initial purpose. No definite characterization could be made about ideological tendencies in 87 (32%) cases. In other words, for nearly 60% of the military coups examined, the political-ideology differential was either absent, neutralized in the short run, or too ambiguous probably to have a great deal of meaning. This generalization pertains to three of the regions, with the exception being the Arab region, where coups are about twice as likely as elsewhere to have definite politically ideological overtones (see Table 12).

Having separated the more or less politically nonideological coups from those with some politically ideological content, Figures 3 through 7 graphically express the aggregate directions of ideational tendencies. It should be noted once again that a coup coalition classified as "more liberal" or "more conservative" is not necessarily very liberal or very conservative and in fact may not even be properly considered "liberal" or "conservative." A conservative coup group that is judged less conservative than the chief executive would be coded as "more liberal." The reader rightly may object to the imprecise nature of the coding. The procedural convolutions only underscore the difficulty of assessing the role of political ideology in the military coup.

Contrary to popular belief, only in Asia do military coups take on a

TABLE 12

POLITICAL IDEOLOGY AND THE MILITARY COUP (in percentages)

		1946-1950	1951-1955	1956-1960	1961-1965	1966-1970	Total
World	(n's)	(43)	(34)	(61)	(77)	(59)	(274)
More Liberal		14	15	18	18	24	18
More Conservative		12	27	26	23	25	23
Total		26	42	44	41	49	41
Absent		12	6	18	18	22	16
Mixed		5	24	7	13	9	11
Ambiguous		57	28	31	28	20	32
Other		74	58	56	59	51	59
Latin America	(n's)	(32)	(26)	(35)	(31)	(12)	(136)
More Liberal		9	8	11	10	17	10
More Conservative		16	31	26	26	17	24
Other		75	61	63	64	66	66
Arab	(n's)	(4)	(5)	(7)	(17)	(16)	(49)
More Liberal		25	60	71	35	44	45
More Conservative		0	0	29	18	31	20
Other		75	40	0	47	25	35
S.E. and E. Asia	(n's)	(5)	(2)	(12)	(14)	(3)	(36)
More Liberal		20	0	8	0	0	6
More Conservative		0	0	25	36	67	28
Other		80	100	67	64	33	66
Sub-Sah. Africa	(n's)	(0)	(0)	(2)	(11)	(25)	(38)
More Liberal		0	0	50	9	20	18
More Conservative		0	0	50	18	20	21
Other		0	0	0	73	60	61

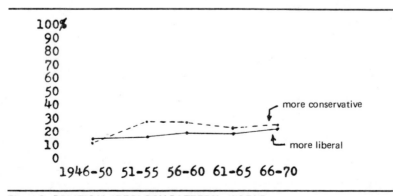

Figure 3: POLITICAL IDEOLOGY PATTERN : WORLD

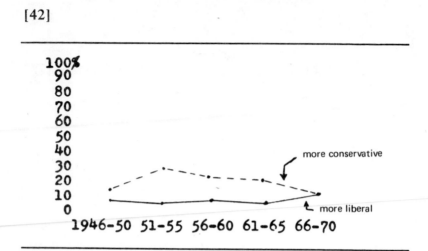

Figure 4: POLITICAL IDEOLOGY PATTERN: LATIN AMERICA

striking conservative flavor. And Asian coups have the highest ambiguity percentage. Latin American coups have been more likely to be more conservative than more liberal until the 1966-1970 period, which witnessed a convergence in ideological patterns, a recent development that presumably will continue at least through the 1970s. Figure 5 reflects the regional preeminence of the Arab variant of socialism and the associated struggles of Nasirite and anti-Nasirite factions. Sub-Saharan African coups are about equally divided. The composite picture, which also reflects South Asia and Europe, demonstrates in Figure 3 an increasing inclination toward the sort of convergence found in the Latin American pattern. The contemporary military coup cannot be categorically defined as either an

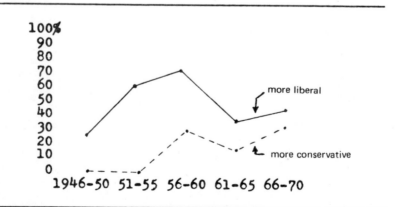

Figure 5: POLITICAL IDEOLOGY PATTERN: ARAB

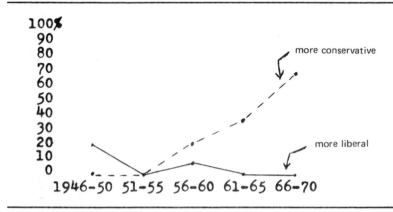

Figure 6: POLITICAL IDEOLOGY PATTERN: S.E. AND E. ASIA

instrument of conservative reaction or of liberal reform. The political ideology dimension is simply not essential to explaining most coups. This should not be surprising in light of the emphasis on corporate and not-so-corporate grievances earlier in this paper. Of those that do exhibit "specific" left-right tendencies, neither the left nor the right proportionately overwhelms the opposite perspective on the status quo. And in a number of these cases, it is erroneous to assume that the coup has come about merely because the executive target is farther left or farther right than the military.[25] Resource and positional threats are generally required in addition to differences of political ideology.

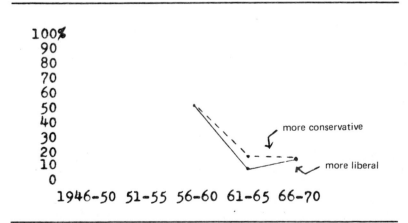

Figure 7: POLITICAL IDEOLOGY PATTERN: SUB SAHARAN AFRICA

Strikingly Reformist

Military coup-makers apparently and primarily are attempting to correct societal injustices and abuses.

For the purposes of this paper, "reform" refers to attempts to correct the injustices and the abuses of the political, social, and economic systems. As such, it may be either liberal or conservative in ideological flavor. Not surprisingly, successful coup-makers rarely omit some appeal to reformist justifications in their post-coup communiques and press conferences. Coup-makers are politicians whether they wear uniforms or not, and one can hardly expect frank discussions of corporate and not-so-corporate interests when it is more discreet to assume the mantle of public interest. Of the 229 coups examined, only 19 were judged to be "strikingly" reformist in nature. "Strikingly" is, to be sure, a subjective modifier. Coup-maker motivations were coded as such when reform was evidently a primary motivation rather than simply a verbal pledge overshadowed by the overt prominence of corporate and not-so-corporate grievances. As it was, 6 of the 19 also involved some corporate factors, 3 served individual positional and resource standings, and 7 entailed personnel adjustments. This section should not be interpreted as arguing that aspiring reformers are not to be found in the other 210 coups. Military coups involve diverse

TABLE 13
"STRIKINGLY" REFORMIST COUPS (in percentages)

	1946-1950	1951-1955	1956-1960	1961-1965	1966-1970	Total
World						
(n's)	(32)	(25)	(55)	(65)	(52)	(229)
%	3	8	9	8	11	8
Latin America						
(n's)	(23)	(17)	(29)	(22)	(10)	(101)
%	0	0	7	5	0	3
Arab						
(n's)	(4)	(5)	(7)	(16)	(14)	(46)
%	25	40	14	6	21	17
S.E. and E. Asia						
(n's)	(4)	(2)	(12)	(13)	(3)	(34)
%	0	0	0	8	0	3
Sub-Sah. Africa						
(n's)	(0)	(0)	(2)	(10)	(22)	(34)
%	0	0	50	0	9	9

coalitions with equally diverse goals. Some segments of the coalition may well be intensely reform oriented, but it would appear that they tend either to be neutralized by more pragmatic coalition partners or to be peripheral to the coup-leadership circle. Even if Table 13 understates the "genuine" reform dimension, it still would be necessary to triple the 19 for strikingly reformist motivations to pertain to even a quarter of the coups examined. Although Table 13 indicates a very slight ascending trend at the coup zone level, one is forced to conclude that the desire for societal reform remains fairly atypical of contemporary military coups.

Order Maintenance

Military coup-makers apparently and primarily are attempting to suppress public disorder for the sake of maintaining public order.

One final category deserves consideration. Rustow (1963: 11) has suggested that military coups commonly follow periods of unrest and disorder. Fossum's (1967: 235) study of successful Latin American coups (1907-1966) reported that 61% were executed during public disorders. More recently, however, Hudson (1970: 281-282) has found that crises of this sort are usually unaccompanied by coups. Additionally, Thompson (1972: 156-157) found that only 29% of the 1946-1970 coups were actually associated with some form of disorder. Of those coups that are immediately preceded by disorder,[26] six possibilities exist to link the coup to the unrest: (1) the timing is coincidental; (2) since the military is very much in demand, the regime is more vulnerable than usual, hence, it is a good opportunity for a coup; (3) the coup-makers are sympathetic to the grievances of the disorderly; (4) the coup-makers fear disorder per se and act to suppress it; (5) the unrest is intended to invite or to provoke a military coup; and (6) some combination of possibilities two through five. Examples can be provided for each of the six, but only the fourth possibility can be readily enumerated. Only 18 coups were judged to have as an apparently primary motive the "neutral" maintenance of public order. While all 18 were successful efforts, the rough trend appears to be the opposite of that found for social reform motivations. Most military coups have less "neutral" sorts of inspiration (see Table 14).

SUMMARY AND CONCLUSIONS

Frequently lacking in much or any apparent ideological or reformist content, coup-maker grievances have two major dimensions: the corporate

TABLE 14
ORDER MAINTENANCE (in percentages)

	1946-1950	1951-1955	1956-1960	1961-1965	1966-1970	Total
World						
(n's)	(32)	(25)	(55)	(65)	(52)	(229)
%	13	4	11	8	4	8
Latin America						
(n's)	(23)	(17)	(29)	(22)	(10)	(101)
%	13	0	7	5	0	6
Arab						
(n's)	(4)	(5)	(7)	(16)	(14)	(46)
%	25	20	0	0	0	4
S.E. and E. Asia						
(n's)	(4)	(2)	(12)	(13)	(3)	(34)
%	0	20	0	8	0	6
Sub-Sah. Africa						
(n's)	(0)	(0)	(2)	(10)	(22)	(34)
%	0	0	50	30	5	15

and the not-so-corporate. As indicated in Table 15, at least eight out of every ten coups involves one or the other or both simultaneously. The corporate dimension encompasses positional/resource conflicts arising within the context of military organizational claims to support, privilege, and boundary maintenance. Ninety-nine coups involved this first issue dimension. The second dimension, the not-so-corporate, encompasses the positional/resource conflicts arising within the context of suborganizational (individual/factional/sectional) claims and subsumes an important subelement: the generalized forms of political warfare exhibited by personnel adjustments. Approximately three of every four coups entailed some form of this second dimension. However, while these dimensions are separable for the purposes of an analytical inventory, in an increasing number of cases, the two general categories overlap in complex and interdependent grievance packages.

The proportional mix of the major motivational dimensions is neither identical for all sectors of the globe nor are the mixes temporally constant. Earlier tables have indicated clear regional differences in the apparent motivational sources of military coups. Figure 8 summarizes in rank order regional grievance propensities. For example, Arab and African coups seem to be those most concerned with corporate positions while Asian and Arab coups are those most concerned with corporate resource standings and

CORPORATE

Position		*Resources*	
1.5	Arab	1	S.E. and E. Asia
1.5	Sub-Sah. Africa	2	Arab
3	Latin America	3	Sub-Sah. Africa
4	S.E. and E. Asia	4	Latin America

NOT-SO-CORPORATE

Individual		*Factional/sectional*	
1	Arab	1	S.E. and E. Asia
2	Latin America	2	Arab
3.5	Sub-Sah. Africa	3	Sub-Sah. Africa
3.5	S.E. and E. Asia	4	Latin America

Personnel adjustments
1 Latin America (preemptive)
2 S.E. and E. Asia (reductionist)
3 Arab (reductionist)
4 Sub-Sah. Africa (reductionist/preemptive)

SOCIETAL RESIDUAL

Strikingly Reformist		*Order Maintenance*	
1	Arab	1	Sub-Sah. Africa
2	Sub-Sah. Africa	2.5	Latin America
3.5	Latin America	2.5	S.E. and E. Asia
3.5	S.E. and E. Asia	4	Arab

SUPPLEMENTARY DATA

Party Alliances		*Electoral Decisions*		*Politically Ideological*	
1	Arab	1	Latin America	1	Arab
2	Latin America	2	Sub-Sah. Africa	2	Sub-Sah. Africa
3	S.E. and E. Asia	3	Arab	3.5	Latin America
4	Sub-Sah. Africa	4	S.E. and E. Asia	3.5	S.E. and E. Asia

Figure 8: REGIONAL DIFFERENCES IN APPARENT COUP MAKER MOTIVATIONAL SOURCES—A SUMMARY

military factional/ethnoregional/sectional interests. In terms of the advancement and the protection of leadership interests (individual), the four regions are not really very dissimilar (see Table 7). The same observation applies to the general category of personnel adjustments; however, the same types of adjustments are not equally experienced in each of the regions.

More generally and with the exception of the Arab world, the not-so-corporate dimension is by far the more common of the two umbrella dimensions (see Table 16). The average ratio of %NSC:%C for

TABLE 15
PROPORTIONAL DISTRIBUTION OF MOTIVATIONAL DIMENSIONS—A SUMMARY (in percentages)

Military Coups Involving:	(n's)	Corporate Motivations	Not-So-Corporate Motivations	Corporate or Not-So-Corporate Motivations	Corporate and Not-So-Corporate Motivations
World					
1946-1950	(32)	31	69	81	19
1951-1955	(25)	44	64	84	24
1956-1960	(55)	35	76	85	25
1961-1965	(65)	49	75	86	37
1966-1970	(52)	52	79	87	44
Total	(229)	43	74	85	32

	World			Latin America			Arab			S.E. and E. Asia			Sub-Sah. Africa		
	(n's)	%C	%NSC	(n's)	%C	%NSC	(n's)	%C	%NSC	(n's)	%C	%NSC	(n's)	%C	%NSC
1946-1950	(32)	31	69	(23)	22	65	(4)	75	50	(4)	25	100	(0)	0	0
1951-1955	(25)	44	64	(17)	47	53	(5)	60	60	(2)	0	100	(0)	0	0
1956-1960	(55)	35	76	(29)	17	69	(7)	29	86	(12)	75	83	(2)	100	50
1961-1965	(65)	49	75	(22)	41	82	(16)	63	69	(13)	54	85	(10)	40	50
1966-1970	(52)	52	79	(10)	30	80	(14)	64	64	(3)	67	67	(22)	45	91
Total	(229)	43	74	(101)	30	70	(46)	59	67	(34)	53	85	(34)	47	76

NOTE: C=corporate and NSC=not-so-corporate.

the coup zone is 1.72. The Asian and African average ratios are very similar to this overall figure. On the other hand, the Arab (1.14) and Latin American (2.33) ratios present clear contrasts. While coup-makers in both regions possess an approximately equal affinity for not-so-corporate motivations, Arab coup-makers have been twice as likely to reflect corporate interests as their Latin American counterparts. Yet, if one examines the change in dimensional mix over time, a slightly different picture emerges. The not-so-corporate element has made relative "gains" in both Latin America and in the Arab world, while the opposite trend is clearly demonstrated by Asian coups. There are, of course, a number of competing hypotheses that could be applied to these differences in regional coup behavior. But one of the more general, if still speculative, observations that can be offered at this time is that one would expect the corporate factors to become distinctively more common in situations where military corporate interests are in the process of being consolidated. A number of Latin American military organizations were far past this stage by 1960 as were, to a lesser extent, several Arab military organizations (e.g., Syria, Egypt, and Iraq). Hence, their grievance-mix ratios tend increasingly to accentuate the not-so-corporate dimension, whereas the trend is reversed for Southeast and East Asia, where corporate consolidation had only begun (with the exception of Thailand) in the late 1950s. The situation of Sub-Saharan Africa is similar to that of Asia in this respect and thus one might expect the African ratio to decline further before rising. At the same time, the clarity of this generalization is clouded by the fact that the three non-Latin American regions are structurally more susceptible to factional/sectional cleavages (see Table 8 and Figure 8) and therefore their respective military organizations are more prone to certain types of not-so-corporate and suborganizational conflicts. In any event, the not-so-corporate motivations virtually are inevitable to coup politics and are not likely to wither away as long as coups continue. Holding other factors constant, the not-so-corporate dimension is probably

TABLE 16
GRIEVANCE MIX RATIOS OVER TIME (%NSC: %C)

	1946-1955	1961-1970	1946-1970
World	67/37=1.81	77/50=1.54	74/43=1.72
Latin America	60/33=1.82	81/38=2.13	70/30=2.33
Arab	56/67= .84	67/63=1.06	67/59=1.14
S.E. and E. Asia	100/17=5.80	81/56=1.45	85/53=1.60
Sub-Sah. Africa	—	78/44=1.77	76/47=1.62

NOTE: NSC = not-so-corporate; C = corporate.

most responsible for the "musical chairs" quality of lengthy coup chains and cycles. Only unusual post-coup leadership and/or outside intervention has been able to repress (but not to eliminate) this proximate source of military-coup motivations.

Finally, two problems stand in the way of providing an adequate assessment of the causal significance of coup-maker grievances. First, this study suffers critically from the lack of data on grievances that did not lead to or at least did not precede military coups. As a result, it could be argued that grievances are simply coincidental to the occurrence of coup events. The possible validity of such a strict interpretation cannot be denied. Yet, given the nonunique nature of coup-maker grievances witnessed by a large and diverse group of qualified observers, the probable validity of the purist's stance seems rather remote. What is even more pertinent, however, is the fully acknowledged inability to approximate the rigor of quantitative models capable of assessing the amount of variance of the dependent variable accounted for by the independent grievance variables. An interim compromise is suggested in Table 17. Each grievance category and subcategory was examined in reference to coup outcomes. Thus, for example, military coups involving "autonomy" grievances were 78% successful. This is not presented as a sophisticated examination, for no controls are applied. But it is interesting to note that coups involving corporate factors are more successful than those involving the not-so-corporate factors. Tentatively then, one might conclude that corporate grievances, while less numerically common, are more potent and thus, in this respect, more salient to the military coup process. That corporate grievances are more potent is additionally supported and partially explained by the fact that the coups in question are more likely to be planned at the highest military levels and to encouter less military resistance.

The second obstacle to a full discourse on the relationship between coup-maker grievances and military coups hinges on the fact that grievances cannot be discussed solely within the micro perspective. Military actors are variably subject to grievances in all political systems and organizational contexts. Nonetheless, all political systems do not experience military coups. This indicates that it is necessary to go beyond the micro focus in order to clarify the causal contribution of coup-maker grievances. Yet, the limitations of space prevent a simultaneous examination of the various macro explanations in this paper. Very briefly, it may be suggested that the grievances are most provocative in situations of regime vulnerability (i.e., where the regime and its leadership is without, has lost, or is in the process of losing alternative [to the military]

TABLE 17
SUCCESS AND THE GRIEVANCES, 1946-1970 (in percentages)

Grievances	% Successful		
Corporate Factors	61		
Corporate Position		73	
Autonomy			78
Hierarchy			90
Monopoly			56
Cohesion			85
Honor			86
Political Position			86
Corporate Resources		57	
Type A			43
Type B			67
Type C			57
Type D			92
Not-So-Corporate Factors	50		
Individual		43	
Factional/Sectional		35	
Military Faction			37
Sectional Group			33
Both			29
Personnel Adjustments		59	
Reductionist			51
Preventive			80
Preservative			100
Preemptive			64
Restorative			11
Societal Residual			
Strikingly Reformist		68	
Order Maintenance		100	

support).[27] The regime-military exchange process—fundamentally the application of force in return for a share of the regime's allocations—becomes asymmetrical in favor of the military. Paradoxically, even as the regime becomes more dependent on its military forces, the likelihood is also increased that various positional and resource values of military actors will be theatened by struggling regime leaders. The basic structural conditions of regime vulnerability thus set a conducive stage for the military coup. But these same structural conditions do not "pull" military coup-makers into direct political action; they are fully capable of marching to their own drums and for their own reasons. Because of that, coup-maker grievances and the proximate perspective advanced in this paper are indispensable to an accurate appreciation of the military coup and the nature of politics in that part of the world currently subject to military coups.

NOTES

1. The first cluster dominates the literature and is actually comprised of five subthematic but not unrelated emphases: (a) *legacies,* see Haddad (1965), Glubb (1966a and 1966b), Johnson (1962, 1964), Gutteridge (1964), O'Connell (1967), and Zinkin (1959); (b) *the failure of democracy,* see Khadduri (1953) and Emerson (1960; (c) *the filling of the void,* see Rustow (1963), Daalder (1962), and Gutteridge (1969); (d) *the middle class spear carriers,* see Halpern (1962), Huntington (1968), and Nun (1967, 1969); (e) *the disjointed system,* see Finer (1962), Rapoport (1962), Huntington (1968), and Perlmutter (1969a). Representatives of the remaining clusters are respectively: (2) Janowitz (1964), Lissak (1967), and Luckham (1971); (3) Huntington (1962), Fossum (1967), Zolberg (1968), and Midlarsky (1970); and (4) Finer (1962), Lieuwen (1964), and Lee (1969).

2. All coups are not military coups. Civilians and irregular and paramilitary formations occasionally act alone. But most coups do require military participation of some sort and it is this participation on which the study is focused. The definition of a military coup does not require that the coup effort be executed exclusively by regular military personnel; only that some regular military personnel participate. Between 1946 and 1970, about two out of every five military coups involved nonregular military actors (e.g., police, paramilitary, and civilians). The one exception was in the case of Panama, where the police, and later, the national guard, have consistently acted as functional equivalents of regular military forces (which are formally absent in Panama) and thus are included in this study.

3. The author's goal is to develop generalized knowledge about military coup behavior as opposed to the tasks of gathering and of analyzing information about one coup or about the coups of one country, several countries, or one geocultural region for a given period of time. Hence, it was decided to study all military coups that could be uncovered within as long a time span as seemed feasible for the resources of a single researcher. The 1947-1970 period met this requirement, although more coups were disclosed than had been originally anticipated. While it is not evident that pre-1946 coups (with the exception that armed forces become less regular the farther back in time one goes) are much different in terms of apparent motivation than post-1945 coups, World War II provided a convenient watershed for them and its consequences did alter the environment in which coups took place. A large number of new and susceptible states had been created. Communist expansion rendered less susceptible some previously susceptible states. And even in Latin America, there was a noticeable decline in the frequency of coups during the early war years, at least until the war's outcome seemed more certain. Furthermore, most of the applicable literature deals with the postwar world, and the breadth of coverage, both journalistic and scholarly, has steadily improved since 1945. This last trend is vital to the validity of the data-making procedures attempted for this paper.

4. Most studies examine only successful coups, primarily for reasons of

convenience. This study collected information on successful, unsuccessful, and compromise military coups. A successful coup requires the removal of the chief executive and a post-coup ruling arrangement satisfactory to the coup-makers. The post-coup ruling arrangement must also survive for at least a week (n=124). Unsuccessful coups must involve a recorded and recognizable physical attempt to seize control (n=131). Without this criterion, it would be impossible to differentiate failures from plots that were crushed, never executed, or manufactured by the regime. Compromise coups may come about in two ways: (1) a chief executive may be removed successfully but resistance to the coup group (as distinguished from defense of the target incumbent) is sufficiently strong to dictate a post-coup ruling arrangement other than that originally envisioned by the coup makers; or, (2) both attacking and defending forces may lack sufficient strength to decide the immediate contest and some interim solution is accepted usually until one or the other gains the upper hand at a later date (n=19). The individual coups are listed in Appendix B.

5. There is no doubt that some coups went undetected. For that matter, an intelligence agency's maxim might be that the only successful coup is the one about which nobody ever hears. The only omission brought to my attention to date was described as an "isolated (Ecuador, 1959) revolt of a small coastal garrison of which very little is known" (Fitch, 1972). In addition to absence of coverage, there also is the possibility that local censors were able to suppress information on unsuccessful attempts. An imperfect test for this bias revealed a measure of association of .24 between a country's coup frequency and its "press freedom score" (Nixon, 1965). The problem with this test is that one would not expect the press to flourish in systems accustomed to military coups. Be that as it may, the statistical relationship is not particularly strong. Nevertheless, the possibility remains quite likely that regimes in states such as Saudi Arabia or Paraguay are able to withhold information on some unsuccessful attempts. Yet, even it this is the case, the possible bias does not seem sufficient to seriously influence this paper's analysis.

6. Grievance information was found to be either unavailable or inadequate for coding purposes for 45 coups (16% of the original n). These were removed from the analysis pool for grievances. A major portion of this discussion is thus based on an n of 229 military coups. An additional bias does arise at this point. Thirty-five (78% of the 45) are Latin American coups while this region has provided only about 50% of the original n. However, the cases in question again are largely obscure and unsuccessful attempts so that the potential for bias should not be exaggerated.

7. All of the source counts in this section could be approximately doubled if "barren" or repetitious sources were to be included. Nor do the source counts take into consideration the material used to make rejection decisions about numerous plots and mutinies. Finally, it should be noted that other coup information (i.e., duration, deaths, participation, and so forth) was sought and the source counts do reflect this aspect of the data collection process.

8. No regional news digest was used for Southeast or East Asia. One does exist (the Asian Recorder) but its contents proved to be more confusing than helpful and consequently it was ignored as a potential source.

9. It also should be noted that the sources were predominantly in the English language. This compounds coverage biases and represents a potential cultural bias in terms of interpretation. At the same time, the various news digests do make selected use of non-English-language newspapers.

10. The sole exception to the "openendedness" involves the item of "anticorrup-

tion" that rarely seemed to possess a great deal of credibility beyond post-coup communiques and yet has become fairly obligatory for these same communiques (see Gutteridge, 1970: 20).

11. Two points need to be made on the coding procedures that were utilized. First, the coder was not required to reconcile differences between different observers (save for such things as dates). This problem might have arisen if a coup had been the subject of several detailed case studies. However, this simply did not happen. If anything, the problem did not arise because few detailed studies are available. The data collector was more in the position of scavenger than that of gourmet. What more likely existed was the situation where one observer would stress one sort of grievance as applicable to a particular coup while another observer would mention other sorts of grievances. In these situations, it was assumed that different observers had perceived different aspects of the same "reality" and both observations were recorded. Second, and fortunately or unfortunately, this project was entirely a one-researcher enterprise. Consequently, no reliability tests, formal or informal, were conducted. To the extent that such tests are necessary to detect disagreement among several coders and related coding instruction problems, reliability tests were not necessary. This does not imply that the data that were subsequently created are perfectly reliable, but only that the question of reliability must await other students who are willing to make use of the same data collection procedures and sources. On the positive side, multiple sources were used to a possibly unprecedented extent and human error was rigorously controlled by triple-checking most of the data-making procedures.

12. In Table 3 and a number of those that follow, the reported data are first aggregated at the world level. Since coup activity is not evenly distributed throughout the world, the reported data also are broken down into the four major regions of military-coup activity: Latin America, Arab, Southeast and East Asia, and Sub-Saharan Africa. Appendix D lists the appropriate members of each region as well as the several states not included in the four regions.

13. Another excellent example is provided by Rotberg's (1971: 157-158) description of the politicization of Haiti's civil-military relations in the late 1930s.

14. This episode is described in Seale (1965: 105).

15. Approaches similar to the "military coup year" have been employed previously by Needler (1968: 61-62) and Hudson (1970: 272). Hopefully, this quite crude technique eventually will be replaced by time-series analysis. This future development must await better data series and an improvement in political scientists' familiarity with the intricacies of sophisticated longitudinal methods.

16. Some analysts will argue that the author has not allowed for a sufficient pre- and post-coup period. The main interest of this primarily descriptive analysis is military coup-maker grievances. A longer pre- and post-period may well yield interesting results, but the farther in time one progresses away from the year of the coup, the less clear is the possible causal interpretation of any results. The situation is not unlike that of interpreting higher order polynomial curves in nonlinear, time-series analysis.

17. From a less proximate perspective, the apparently weak association between coups and defense budget fluctuations is supported by an ordinal and bivariate examination of measures of association between military-coup proneness (a system is considered more coup prone if it experiences a military coup during the appropriate time periods and less coup prone if no coup occurs) and absolute defense

expenditures, defense expenditures/armed forces personnel, and defense expenditures/governmental budgets, with a near universal n. The measures of association (Somers D) were weakly negative for the first two expenditure variables and very weakly positive for the third (see Thompson, 1972: 164). On the other hand, using Bank's (1971: 99-136) incomplete data on relative defense budgets, the 1965 mean for states that experienced military coups during 1946-1970 is 22.2% (n=33; range=.32 – 48.9%). The mean for states that had not experienced military coups is 13.1% (n=38; range=0.0 – 42.0%). The average difference is nearly 10%. Furthermore, Modelski (1972: 132) has suggested that fluctuations in the "global militarization index" (gross world product/world military expenditures) might have an important relationship with the rate of military coups. Preliminary investigation of this hypothesis has yielded an impressive Pearson correlation of .68 for the period 1961-1970. While these latter findings do not necessarily conflict with the more proximate arguments and findings discussed in this paper, they do suggest that a total denial of any link between coups and military expenditures is not warranted at this time. The problem definitely merits further consideration.

18. Vatikiotis' (1967: 174) observation that war defeats are "the most common accelerator of coups" does not appear to be substantiated by the 1946-1970 data.

19. This is a highly confusing period in Argentina's political history. Springer (1968) is recommended for those desiring more information.

20. However, the ultimate political expression of primordial groups, separatism, is extremely rare in connection with military coups. Only five coups have had separatist goals and these have been confined to Indonesia, Zaire, Nigeria, and Syria. The Syrian case differs from the rest in that it entailed the severing of Syria from membership in the United Arab Republic. The other four cases eventually were unsuccessful and, with the exception of the Zaire event (1967), were extremely lethal for they escalated beyond the behavioral parameters of the conventional military coup.

21. Not surprisingly, in only about five or six cases have alliances been made with Communist parties. At least two of these cases (Venezuela, 1962) were apparently instances of Communists seizing the opportunity provided by the coup activity and may not have been in actual alliance with the military conspirators.

22. Riker (1962) has generalized this process by proposing that winning coalitions will seek to reduce their size to that of minimally winning coalitions. Quandt (1969: 162-163) provides an illuminating discussion of this principle in terms of Algerian coalition behavior. Riggs (1966: 215-216) describes what might be called the "khana (coup group) syndrome" in Thai politics, which is essentially a similar process. See also Thibaut and Kelly's (1959: 215) earlier formulation.

23. This account of Algerian politics concentrates on coup-coalition reduction. Other factors were naturally involved in each of the five coups. For a more complete analysis, see the works of Quandt (1969), Ottoway and Ottoway (1970), and Zartman (1970).

24. For that matter, Canton (1969: 256-257), in a study of Argentinian military revolts between 1900 and 1966, found that no revolt favorable to a popular party was ever successful and that most of the revolts against popular parties were successful.

25. James Payne (1968: 155) has made this same point in reference to Latin American coups.

26. Bienen (1968: 35) defines public order as "a stable situation in which the

security of individuals or groups is not threatened and in which disputes are settled without resort to violence." Public disorder is then the reverse situation, that of unrest and the deterioration of general security.

27. Regime vulnerability situations are, in turn, variously but by no means overwhelmingly associated with: (a) a previous history of regime vulnerability, (b) a number of systemic indicators (e.g., levels of economic development and social mobilization) which measure background conditions related to the development of alternative regime support relationships, and (c) processes of deterioration in terms of economic welfare, public order, and regime performance.

REFERENCES

Africa Diary (1966) Vol. 6 (July 25-31): 2963-2964.

AFRIFA, A. A. (1966) The Ghana Coup. London: Frank Cass.

ALEXANDER, R. J. (1970) "Bolivia: The national revolution," in M. C. Needler (ed.) Political Systems of Latin America. 2d ed.

——— (1964) The Venezuelan Democratic Revolution: A Profile of the Regime of Romulo Betancourt. New Brunswick: Rutgers Univ. Press.

——— (1958a) "The army in politics," in H. E. Davis (ed.) Government and Politics in Latin America. New York: Ronald Press.

——— (1958b) The Bolivian National Revolution. New Brunswick: Rutgers Univ. Press.

ANDERSON, C. W. (1970a) "El Salvador: the army as reformer," in M. C. Needler (ed.) Political Systems of Latin America. 2d ed. New York: Van Nostrand Reinhold.

——— (1970b) Honduras: problems of an apprentice democracy," in M. C. Needler (ed.) Political Systems of Latin America. 2d ed. New York: Van Nostrand Reinhold.

ANDRESKI, S. (1968) Military Organization and Society. 2nd ed. Berkeley: Univ. of California Press.

——— (1961) "Conservatism and radicalism of the military." Eur. J. of Soc. 2,1.

ASTIZ, C. A. (1969) "The Argentine armed forces: their role and political involvement." West. Pol. Q. 22,4.

AVERY, P. (1965) Modern Iran. New York: Frederick A. Praeger.

BANKS, A. S. (1971) Cross-Polity Time-Series Data. Cambridge: MIT Press.

BARAGER, J. R. (1970) "Argentina: a country divided," in M. C. Needler (ed.) Political Systems of Latin America. 2d ed. New York: Van Nostrand Reinhold.

BAYNE, E. A. (1969) "Somalia's myths are tested." A.V.F.S. Northeast Africa Series 16,1 (October).

BE'ERI, E. (1970) Army Officers in Arab Politics and Society. New York: Praeger.

BELL, J. B. (1970) "Southern Yemen: two years of independence." World Today 26,2 (February).

BELL, M.J.V. (1965) "Army and nation in Sub-Saharan Africa." Adelphi Papers, no. 21. London: Institute for Strategic Studies.

BELTRAN, V. R. (1968) "The army and structural changes in 20th century

Argentina: an initial approach," in J. Van Doorn (ed.) Armed Forces and Society: Sociological Essays. The Hague: Mouton.

BIENEN, H. (1968) "Public order and the military in Africa: mutinies in Kenya, Uganda, and Tanganyika," in H. Bienen (ed.) The Military Intervenes: Case Studies in Political Development. New York: Russell Sage.

BLANKSTEN, G. I. (1970) "Ecuador: the politics of instability," in M. C. Needler (ed.) Political Systems of Latin America. 2d ed. New York: Van Nostrand Reinhold.

––– (1951) Ecuador: Constitutions and Caudillos. Univ. of California Publications in Political Science, 3,1. Berkeley: Univ. of California Press.

BRACKMAN, A. C. (1969) The Communist Collapse in Indonesia. New York: W. W. Norton.

BRILL, W. H. (1967) Military Intervention in Bolivia: The Overthrow of Paz Estenssoro and MNR. Political Studies Series, no. 3. Washington: Institute for the Comparative Study of Political Systems.

BUTTINGER, J. (1967) Vietnam: A Dragon Embattled: Vietnam at War. Vol. 2. New York: Frederick A. Praeger.

BUTWELL, R. A. (1963) Univ. of Burma. Stanford: Stanford Univ. Press.

CALVERT, P.A.R. (1969) Latin America: Internal Conflict and International Peace. New York: St. Martin's Press.

CAMPBELL, J. and P. SHERRARD (1968) Modern Greece. New York: Frederick A. Praeger.

CANTON, D. (1969) "Military intervention in Argentina: 1900-1966," in J. Van Doorn (ed.) Military Profession and Military Regimes: Commitments and Conflicts. The Hague: Mouton.

CARLETON, A. (1950) "The Syrian coups d'état of 1949." Middle East J. 4,1 (January).

CLAPHAM, C. (1968) "The Ethiopian coup d'état of December, 1960." J. of Mod. African Studies 6,4.

COTTAM, R. W. (1964) Nationalism in Iran. Pittsburgh: Univ. of Pittsburgh Press.

"B. D." (1952) "Political alarms in Bangkok." World Today 8,2 (February).

DAALDER, H. (1962) The Role of the Military in the Emerging Countries. The Hague: Mouton.

DALBY, D. (1967) "The military take-over in Sierra Leone." World Today 23,8 (August).

DANN, V. (1969) Iraq Under Qassem: A Political History, 1958-1963. New York: Praeger.

DIX, R. H. (1967) Colombia: The Political Dimensions of Change. New Haven: Yale Univ. Press.

DOMMEN, A. J. (1964) Conflict in Laos: The Politics of Neutralization. New York: Frederick A. Praeger.

DONNISON, F.S.V. (1970) Burma. New York: Praeger.

DUBOIS, V. D. (1969) "The struggles for stability in the Upper Volta—part III; the fall of Maurice Yameogo." A.V.F.S. West Africa Series, no. 3 (March).

DULLES, J.W.F. (1970) Unrest in Brazil: Political-Military Crises, 1955-1964. Austin: Univ. of Texas Press.

DUNCANSON, D. J. (1968) Government and Revolution in Vietnam. New York: Oxford Univ. Press.

DUPREE, L. (1969) "The military is dead! long live the military!" A.V.F.S. South Asia Series 13,3 (April).

DUPUY, T. N. (1961) "Burma and its army: a contrast in motivations and characteristics." Antioch Rev. 20,4 (Winter).

ECKSTEIN, H. (1965) "On the etiology of internal wars." History and Theory 4,2.

EINAUDI, L. R. (1969) "The Peruvian military: a summary political analysis." (RM-60480RC) Santa Monica: RAND.

EMERSON, R. (1960) From Empire to Nation. Boston: Beacon.

FAGG, J. E. (1965) Cuba, Haiti, and the Dominican Republic. Englewood Cliffs, N.J.: Prentice-Hall.

FALL, B. B. (1969) Anatomy of a Crisis: The Laotian Crisis of 1960-1961. R. M. Smith (ed.) Garden City, N.Y.: Doubleday.

FEITH, H. (1962) The Decline of Constitutional Democracy in Indonesia. Ithaca: Cornell Univ. Press.

--- and D. S. LEV (1963) "The end of the Indonesian rebellion." Pacific Affairs 36, 1 (Spring).

FERNS, H. S. (1969) Argentina. New York: Praeger.

FINER, S. E. (1962) The Man on Horseback: The Role of the Military in Politics. London: Pall Mall Press.

FIRST, R. (1970) The Barrel of a Gun: Political Power in Africa and the Coup d'Etat. London: Penguin Press.

FISHER, H. J. (1969) "Elections and coups in Sierra Leone, 1967." J. of Mod. African Studies 7,4 (December).

FITCH, J. S. III. (1972) Personal correspondence with author (May 5).

FLUHARTY, V. L. (1957) Dance of the Millions: Military Rule and the Social Revolution on Colombia, 1930-1956. Pittsburgh: Univ. of Pittsburgh Press.

FOSSUM, E. (1967) "Factors influencing the occurrence of military coups d'état in Latin America." J. of Peace Res. 3.

GALBRAITH, W. O. (1966) Colombia: A General Survey. 2d ed. London: Oxford Univ. Press.

GALLO, E. (1969) "Argentina: background to the present crisis." World Today 25,11 (November).

GARIN, C. (1970) "Dahomey: another coup." Africa Report 15,1 (January).

GLUBB, J. B. (1966a) "The conflict between tradition and modernism in the role of Muslim armies," in C. Leiden (ed.) The Conflict of Traditionalism and Modernism in the Muslim Middle East. Austin: Univ. of Texas.

--- (1966b) "The role of the army in the traditional Arab State," in J. H. Thompson and R. D. Reischauer (eds.) Modernization of the Arab World. Princeton: D. Van Nostrand.

GOLDRICH, D. (1970) "Panama," in M. C. Needler (ed.) Political Systems of Latin America. New York: Van Nostrand Reinhold.

GREENFIELD, R. (1965) Ethiopia: A New Political History. New York: Frederick A. Praeger.

GRUNDY, K. W. (1968) Conflicting Images of the Military in Africa. Short Studies and Reprint Series: Dept. of Political Science and Public Administration, Makere Univ. College. Kampala (Uganda): East Africa Publishing House.

GURR, T. R. (1970) Why Men Rebel. Princeton: Princeton Univ. Press.

GUTTERIDGE, W. (1970) "Why does an African army take power?" Africa Report 15,7 (October).

--- (1969) The Military in African Politics. London: Methuen.

--- (1964) Military Institutions and Power in the New States. London: Pall Mall Press.

HADDAD, G. M. (1971) Revolutions and Military Rule in the Middle East: The Arab States: Iraq, Syria, Lebanon, and Jordan. New York: Robert Speller.
——— (1965) Revolutions and Military Rule in the Middle East: The Northern Tier. New York: Robert Speller.
HALPERN, M. (1963) The Politics of Social Change in the Middle East and North Africa. Princeton: Princeton Univ. Press.
HARRIS, G. S. (1965) "The role of the military in Turkish Politics, Part II." Middle East J. 19,2 (Spring).
HENDERSON, G. (1968) Korea: The Politics of the Vortex. Cambridge: Harvard Univ. Press.
HENDERSON, K.D.D. (1965) Sudan Republic. London: Ernest Benn.
HENNESSY, A. (1970) "Cuba: the politics of frustrated nationalism," in M. C. Needler (ed.) Political Systems of Latin America. 2d ed. New York: Van Nostrand Reinhold.
HINDLEY, D. (1968) "Indonesian politics, 1965-7: the September 30 movement and the fall of Sukarno." World Today 24,8 (August).
HOLT, P. M. (1963) A Modern History of the Sudan. New York: Frederick A. Praeger.
HUDSON, M. C. (1970) Conditions of Political Violence and Instability: A Preliminary Test of Three Hypotheses. Sage Professional Papers in Comparative Politics, Vol. 1. H. Eckstein and T. R. Gurr (eds.) Beverly Hills: Sage Pubns.
——— (1968) The Precarious Republic: Modernization in Lebanon. New York: Random House.
HUMBRACI, A. (1966) Algeria: A Revolution That Failed. New York: Frederick A. Praeger.
HUNTINGTON, S. P. (1968) Political Order in Changing Societies. New Haven: Yale Univ. Press.
——— (1962) "Patterns of violence in world politics," in S. P. Huntington (ed.) Changing Patterns of Military Politics, Vol. 3 of International Yearbook of Political Behavior Research. Glencoe, Ill.: Free Press.
INGRAMS, H. (1964) The Yemen: Imams, Rulers, and Revolutions. New York: Frederick A. Praeger.
JANOWITZ, M. (1964) The Military in the Political Development of New Nations: An Essay in Comparative Analysis: Chicago: Univ. of Chicago Press.
JOHNSON, J. J. (1964) The Military and Society in Latin America. Stanford: Stanford Univ. Press.
——— (1962) "The Latin American military as a politically competing group in transitional society," in J. J. Johson (ed.) The Role of the Military in Underdeveloped Countries. Princeton: Princeton Univ. Press.
JOHNSON, K. F. with M. M. FUERTES, and P. L. PARIS (1969) Argentina's Mosaic of Discord, 1966-1968. Political Studies Series, no. 6. Washington: Institute for the Comparative Study of Political Systems.
JOSHI, B. L. and L. E. ROSE, (1966) Democratic Innovations in Nepal: A Case Study of Political Acculturation. Berkeley: Univ. of California Press.
JUMPER, R. and M. W. NORMAND. (1964) "Vietnam," in G. M. Kahin (ed.) Government and Politics of Southeast Asia. Ithaca: Cornell Univ. Press.
KAHIN, G. M. and J. W. LEWIS (1969) The United States in Vietnam. Rev. ed. New York: Dial Press.

Keesing's Contemporary Archives (1968) Vol. 16 (April 6-13): 22633-22634.

KELLY, G. A. (1965) Lost Soldiers: The French Army and Empire in Crisis, 1947-1962. Cambridge: MIT Press.

KHADDURI, M. (1969a) "Iraq, 1958 and 1963," in W. G. Andrews and U. Ra'anan (eds.) The Politics of the Coup d'Etat. New York: Van Nostrand Reinhold.

――― (1969b) Republican Iraq. London: Oxford Univ. Press.

――― (1963) "The role of the military in Iraqi society," in S. N. Fisher (ed.) The Military in the Middle East. Columbus: Ohio State Univ. Press.

――― (1953) "The role of the military in Middle East politics." Amer. Pol. Sci. Rev. 48,2 (June).

――― (1952) "Coup and counter-coup in the Yaman, 1948." International Affairs (London) 28,1 (January).

KILNER, P. (1959) "A year of army rule in the Sudan." World Today 15,11 (November).

KIM, C.I.E. (1968) "The South Korean military coup of May, 1961: its causes and the social characteristics of its leaders," in J. Van Doorn (ed.) Armed Forces and Society: Sociological essay. The Hague: Mouton.

KIRK-GREENE, A.H.M. (1971) Crisis and Conflict in Nigeria: A Documentary Sourcebook, 1966-69. Vol. 1, January, 1966 – July, 1967. London: Oxford Univ. Press.

KLING, M. (1962) "Towards a theory of power and political instability in Latin America," in J. H. Kautsky (ed.) Political Change in Underdeveloped Countries: Nationalism and Communism. New York: John Wiley.

KRAUS, J. (1970) "Arms and politics in Ghana," in C. E. Welch, Jr. (ed.) Soldier and State in Africa: A Comparative Analysis of Military Intervention and Political Change. Evanston: Northwestern Univ. Press.

――― (1969) "Ghana, 1966," in W. G. Andrews and U Ra'anan (eds.) The Politics of the Coup d'Etat. New York: Van Nostrand Reinhold.

――― (1966) "The men in charge." Africa Report 11,4 (April).

LANG, K. (1968) "The military putsch in a developed political culture: confrontations of military and civil power in Germany and France," in J. Van Doorn (ed.) Armed Forces and Society: Sociological Essays. The Hague: Mouton.

LEE, J. M. (1969) African Armies and Civil Order. Institute for Strategic Studies: Studies in International Security, no. 13. New York: Praeger.

LEFEVER, E. W. (1970) Spear and Sceptre: Army, Police, and Politics in Tropical Africa. Washington: Brookings Institution.

LEGG, K. R. (1969) Politics in Modern Greece. Stanford: Stanford Univ. Press.

LEGVOLD, R. (1970) Soviet Policy in West Africa. Cambridge: Harvard Univ. Press.

LEIFER, M. (1970) "Political upheaval in Cambodia." World Today 26,5 (May).

LEMARCHAND, R. (1968) "Dahomey: coup within a coup." Africa Report 13,6 (June).

――― (1967) "The passing of mwamiship in Burundi." Africa Report 12,1 (January).

LENCZOWSKI, G. (1965) "Iraq: seven years of revolution." Current History 48,285 (May).

LEVINE, D. N. (1968) "The military in Ethiopian politics: capabilities and constraints," in H. Bienen (ed.) The Military Intervenes: Case Studies in Political Development. New York: Russell Sage.

LEVINE, V. T. (1968) "The coup in the Central African Republic." Africa Today 15,2 (April-May).

——— (1967) "Independent Africa in trouble." Africa Report 12,9 (December).

LEWIS, W. H. (1966) "The decline of Algeria's FLN." Middle East J. 20,2 (Spring).

LIEUWEN, E. (1965) Venezuela. 2d ed. London: Oxford Univ. Press.

——— (1964) Generals Vs. Presidents: Neo-Militarism in Latin America. New York: Frederick A. Praeger.

LISSAK, M. (1967) "Modernization and role expansion of the military in developing countries." Comparative Studies in Society and History 9,3 (April).

LLOYD, P. C. (1967) Africa in Social Change. New York: Frederick A. Praeger.

LOGAN, R. W. (1968) Haiti and the Dominican Republic. New York: Oxford Univ. Press.

LOTT, L. B. (1970) "Venezuela," in M. C. Needler (ed.) Political Systems of Latin America. 2d ed. New York: Van Nostrand Reinhold.

LUCKHAM, A. R. (1971) "A comparative typology of civil-military relations." Government and Opposition 6, 1 (Winter).

MACK, R. W. and R. C. SNYDER (1957) "The analysis of social conflict: toward an overview and synthesis." J. of Conflict Res. 1 (June).

MALLOY, J. M. (1970) Bolivia: The Uncompleted Revolution. Pittsburgh: Univ. of Pittsburgh Press.

MARCH, R. W. and R. C. SNYDER (1957) "The analysis of social conflict: toward an overview and synthesis." J. of Conflict Res. 1 (June).

MARRETT, R. (1969) Peru. New York: Praeger.

MARTZ, J. D. (1962) Colombia: A Contemporary Political Survey. Chapel Hill: Univ. of North Carolina Press.

——— (1959) Central America: The Crisis and the Challenge. Chapel Hill: Univ. of North Carolina Press.

MEISEL, J. H. (1962) The Fall of the Republic: Military Revolt in France. Ann Arbor: Univ. of Michigan Press.

MENARD, O. D. (1967) The Army and the French Republic. Lincoln: Univ. of Nebraska Press.

MENNINGER, K. with M. MAYMAN and P. PRUYSER (1963) The Vital Balance: The Life Process in Mental Health and Illness. New York: Viking Press.

MIDLARSKY, M. (1970) "Mathematical models of instability and a theory of diffusion." Int. Studies Q. 14,1 (March).

MODELSKI, G. (1972) Principles of World Politics. New York: Free Press.

MORENO, J. A. (1970) "Chronology of events relevant to the April revolution," in R. R. Fagen and W. A. Cornelius, Jr. (ed.) Political Power in Latin America: Seven Confrontations. Englewood Cliffs, N.J.: Prentice-Hall.

——— (1967) "Sociological aspects of the Dominican revolution." Ithaca: Cornell University Latin American Studies Program Dissertation Series.

NEEDLER, M. C. (1968) Political Development in Latin America: Instability, Violence, and Evolutionary Change. New York: Random House.

——— (1964) Anatomy of a Coup d'Etat: Educator, 1963. Special Article Series, no. 1. Washington: Institute for the Comparative Study of Political Systems.

NELKIN, D. (1967) "The economic and social setting of military takeovers in Africa." J. of Asian and African Studies 2, 3-4 (July and October).

NIVEN, R. (1967) Nigeria. New York: Frederick A. Praeger.

NIXON, R. F. (1965) "Freedom in the world's press: a fresh appraisal with new data." Journalism Q. 42,1 (Winter).

NORDLINGER, E. A. (1970) "Soldiers in mufti: the impact of military rule upon economic and social change in the nonwestern states." Amer. Pol. Sci. Rev. 64,4 (December).

NORTH, L. (1966) Civil-Military Relations in Argentina, Chile, and Peru. Politics of Modernization Studies. Berkeley: Institute of International Studies.

NUN, J. (1969) Latin America: The Hegemonic Crisis and the Military Coup. Politics of Modernization Series, no. 7. Berkeley: Institute ot International Studies.

--- (1967) "The middle class military coup," in C. Veliz (ed.) The Politics of Conformity in Latin America. London: Oxford Univ. Press.

O'Ballance, E. (1971) The War in the Yemen. Hamden: Anchor Books.

O'BALLANCE, E. (1971) The War in the Yemen. Hamden: Anchor Books. Modern African Studies 5,2.

OH, J. K. (1968) Korea: Democracy on Trial. Ithaca: Cornell Univ. Press.

OTTAWAY, D. and M. OTTAWAY, (1970) Algeria: The Politics of a Socialist Revolution. Berkeley: Univ. of California Press.

OZBUDUN, E. (1966) The Role of the Military in Recent Turkish Politics. Occasional Papers in International Affairs, no. 14. Cambridge: Harvard University Center for International Affairs.

PAPANDREOU, A. (1970) Democracy at Gunpoint: The Greek Front. Garden City, N.Y.: Doubleday.

PARKER, F. D. (1964) The Central American Republics. London: Oxford Univ. Press.

PATAI, R. (1958) The Kingdom of Jordan. Princeton: Princeton Univ. Press.

PATCH, R. W. (1959) "The Bolivian falange: a letter from Richard W. Patch." A.U.F.S. West Coast South American Series 6,4 (April).

PAYNE, A. (1968) The Peruvian Coup D'Etat of 1962: The Overthrow of Manuel Prado. Political Studies Series, no. 5. Washington: Institute for the Comparative Study of Political Systems.

PAYNE, J. L. (1968) Patterns of Conflict in Colombia. New Haven: Yale Univ. Press.

PENDLE, G. (1963) Argentina. London: Oxford Univ. Press.

PERLMUTTER, A. (1969a) "The Praetorian state and the Praetorian army." Comparative Politics 3 (April).

--- (1969b) "From obscurity to rule: the Syrian army and the Ba'th party." West. Pol. Q. 22,4 (December).

PETERSON, P. (1970) "Brazil: revolution or reaction?" in M. C. Needler (ed.) Political Systems of Latin America. 2d ed. New York: Van Nostrand Reinhold.

PIKE, F. B. (1967) The Modern History of Peru. New York: Frederick A. Praeger.

POPPINO, R. E. (1966) "Brazil since 1954," in J. M. Bello (ed.) A History of Modern Brazil, 1889-1964. Trans. by J. L. Taylor. Stanford: Stanford Univ. Press.

PRICE, R. M. (1971) "Military officers and political leadership: the Ghanaian case." Comparative Politics 3,3 (April).

QUANDT, W. B. (1969) Revolution and Political Leadership: Algeria, 1954-1968. Cambridge: MIT Press.

RAPOPORT, D. C. (1962) "A comparative theory of military and political types," in S. P. Huntington (ed.) Changing Patterns of Military Politics. Glencoe, Ill.: Free Press.

RIGGS, F. W. (1966) Thailand, The Modernization of a Bureaucratic Polity. Honolulu: East-West Center Press.

RIKER, W. H. (1962) The Theory of Political Coalitions. New Haven: Yale Univ. Press.

ROSS, S. R. (1956) "Some observations on military coups in the Caribbean," in A. C. Wingus (ed.) The Caribbean: Its Political Problems. Gainesville: Univ. of Florida Press.

ROTBERG, R. I. with C. K. CLAGUE (1971) Haiti, the Politics of Squalor. Boston: Houghton Mifflin.

ROTH, G. (1968) "Personal rulership, patrimonialism, and empire-building in the new states." World Politics 20,2 (January).

ROWE, J. W. (1964a) "Revolution or counterrevolution in Brazil? An interim assessment of the 'April movement'. Part I, The diverse background." A.U.F.S. East Coast South Amer. Series 11,4 (June).

––– (1964b) "Revolution or counterrevolution in Brazil? An interim assessment of the 'April movement.' Part II: From "black Friday" to the new reforms." A.U.F.S. East Coast South Amer. Series 12,7 (November).

RUSTOW, D. A. (1963) "The military in Middle Eastern society and politics," in S. N. Fisher (ed.) The Military in the Middle East. Columbus: Ohio State Univ. Press.

AL-SADAT, A. (1957) Revolt on the Nile. New York: John Day.

"S. H." (1949) "Musical chairs in Siam." World Today 5,9 (September).

SAYEED, K. B. (1967) The Political System of Pakistan. Boston: Houghton Mifflin.

SCHMIDT, D. A. (1968) Yemen, The Unknown War. New York: Holt, Rinehart & Winston.

SCHMITT, K. M. and D. D. BURKS (1963) Evolution or Chaos: Dynamics of Latin American Government and Politics. New York: Frederick A. Praeger.

SEALE, P. (1965) The Struggle for Syria: A Study of Post-War Politics, 1945-1958. London: Oxford Univ. Press.

SHAPLEN, R. (1969) Time Out of Hand: Revolution and Reaction in Southeast Asia. New York: Harper & Row.

––– (1965) The Lost Revolution. New York: Harper & Row.

SHWADRAN, B. (1960) The Power Struggle in Iraq. New York: Council for Middle Eastern Affairs Press.

SILVERSTEIN, J. (1964) "Burma," in G. M. Kahin (ed.) Governments and Politics of Southeast Asia. 2d ed. Ithaca: Cornell Univ. Press.

SIPRI (1971) The Arms Trade with the Third World, Stockholm International Peace Research Institute. Stockholm: Almqvist and Wiksell.

SKIDMORE, T. E. (1967) Politics in Brazil, 1930-1964: An Experiment in Democracy. London: Oxford Univ. Press.

SKURNIK, W.A.E. (1970) "The military and politics: Dahomey and Upper Volta," in C. E. Welch, Jr. (ed.) Soldier and State in Africa. Evanston: Northwestern Univ. Press.

––– (1968) "Dahomey: the end of a military regime." Africa Today 15, 2 (April-May).

SMITH, R. (1964) "Laos," in G. M. Kahin (ed.) Governments and Politics of Southeast Asia. 2d ed. Ithaca: Cronell Univ. Press.

SOHN, J. S. (1968) "Political dominance and political failure; the role of the military in the Republic of Korea," in H. Bienen (ed.) The Military Intervenes: Case Studies in Political Development. New York: Russell Sage.

SPRINGER, P. B. (1968) "Disunity and disorder: factional politics in the Argentine military," in H. Bienen (ed.) The Military Intervenes: Case Studies in Political Development. New York: Russell Sage.

STEPAN, A. (1971) The Military in Politics: Changing Patterns in Brazil. Princeton: Princeton Univ. Press.

STEPHENS, I. (1963) Pakistan. New York: Frederick A. Praeger.

STOKES, W. S. (1959) Latin American Politics. New York: Thomas Y. Crowell.

STONE, L. (1966) "Theories of revolution." World Politics 18,2 (January).

STRICKLAND, D. A., L. L. WADE, and R. E. JOHNSTON (1968) A Primer of Political Analysis. Chicago: Markham.

TAYLOR, P. B. Jr. (1968) The Venezuelan Golpe de Estado of 1958: The Fall of Marcos Perex Jimenez. Political Studies Series, no. 4. Washington: Institute for the Comparative Study of Political Systems.

THIBAUT, J. W. and H. H. KELLEY (1959) The Social Psychology of Groups. New York: John Wiley.

THOMAS, H. (1971) Cuba, The Pursuit of Freedom. New York: Harper & Row.

THOMPSON, W. R. (1972) Explanations of the Military Coup. Ph.D. dissertation. Seattle: Univ. of Washington. (unpublished)

TORREY, G. H. (1964) Syrian Politics and the Military, 1945-1958. Columbus: Ohio State Univ. Press.

––– (1963) "The role of the military in society and government and the formation of the U.A.R.," in S. N. Fisher (ed.) The Military in the Middle East. Columbus: Ohio State Univ. Press.

TRAGER, F. N. (1963) "The failure of U Nu and the return of the armed forces in Burma." Rev. of Pol. 25,3 (July).

ULMAN, A. H. and F. TACHAU (1965) "Turkish politics: the attempt to reconcile rapid modernization with democracy." Middle East J. 19,2 (Spring).

VATIKIOTIS, P. J. (1969) The Modern History of Egypt. New York: Praeger.

––– (1968) "Some political consequences of the 1952 revolution in Egypt," in P. M. Holt (ed.) Political and Social Change in Modern Egypt: Historical Studies From the Ottoman Conquest to the United Arab Republic. London: Oxford Univ. Press.

––– (1967) Politics and the Military in Jordan: A Study of the Arab Legion, 1921-1957. London: Frank Cass.

––– (1961) The Egyptian Army in Politics: Pattern for New Nations? Bloomington: Indiana Univ. Press.

WEEKS, R. V. (1964) Pakistan: Birth and Growth of a Muslim Nation. Princeton: D. Van Nostrand.

WEIKER, W. F. (1963) The Turkish Revolution, 1960-61. Washington: Brookings Institution.

WELCH, C. A. Jr., (1970) "The roots and implications of military intervention," in C. E. Welch, Jr. (ed.) Soldier and State in Africa. Evanston, Ill.: Northwestern Univ. Press.

WENNER, M. W. (1970) "The people's republic of South Yemen," in T. Y. Ismael (ed.) Govements and Politics of the Contemporary Middle East. Homewood, Ill.: Dorsey Press.

––– (1967) Modern Yemen, 1918-1966. Baltimore: Johns Hopkins Press.

WESSON, R. G. (1967) The Imperial Order. Berkeley: Univ. of California Press.

WIARDA, H. J. (1969) The Dominican Republic: Nation in Transition. New York: Praeger.

––– (1968a) "The politics of civil-military relations in the Dominican Republic." J. of Inter-American Studies 7,4.

––– (1968b) Dictatorship and Development: The Methods of Control in Trujillo's Dominican Republic. Gainesville: Univ. of Florida Press.

WILCOX, W. A. (1965) "The Pakistan coup d'état of 1958." Pacific Affairs 38, 2 (Summer).

WILLIAME, J. C. (1970) "Congo-Kinshasa: General Mobutu and two political generations," in C. E. Welch, Jr. (ed.) Soldier and State in Africa. Evanston: Northwestern Univ. Press.

WILSON, D. A. (1964) "Thailand," in G. M. Kahin (ed.) Governments and Politics of Southeast Asia. 2d ed. Ithaca: Cornell Univ. Press.

——— (1962) Politics in Thailand. Ithaca: Cornell Univ. Press.

YALMAN, N. (1968) "Intervention and extrication: the officer corps in the Turkish crisis," in H. Bienen (ed.) The Military Intervenes: Case Studies in Political Development. New York: Russell Sage.

YOUNG, C. (1965) Politics in the Congo: Decolonization and Independence. Princeton: Princeton Univ. Press.

ZARTMAN, I. W. (1970) "The Algerian army in politics," in C. E. Welch, Jr. (ed.) Soldier and State in Africa. Evanston: Northwestern Univ. Press.

ZIADEH, N. A. (1957) Syria and Lebanon. New York: Frederick A. Praeger.

ZINKIN, T. (1959) "India and military dictatorship." Pacific Affairs 32,1 (March).

ZIRING, L. (1971) The Ayub Khan Era: Politics in Pakistan, 1958-1969. Syracuse: Syracuse Univ. Press.

ZOLBERG, A. R. (1969) "Military Rule and Political Development in tropical Africa: a preliminary report," in J. Van Doorn (ed.) Military Profession and Military Regimes: Commitments and Conflicts. The Hague: Mouton.

——— (1968) "Military intervention in the new states of tropical Africa: elements of comparative analysis," in H. Bienen (ed.) The Military Intervenes: Case Studies in Political Development. New York: Russell Sage.

MILITARY COUP-MAKER GRIEVANCES: CODING DEFINITIONS

CORPORATE

Corporate Positions

Military coup-makers apparently perceive a threat to:

autonomy—the military's scope of independent control over its general organizational activities.

hierarchy—the military's organization chain of command.

monopoly—the military's functional claim to existence as the nation-state's principal, legitimate organization of armed force.

cohesion—the military's organizational unity.

honor—the military's collective self-esteem.

political position—the military's organizational relationship with the political system. The relationship will fall somewhere on an abstract continuum ranging from the one extreme of complete dominance of the political system to the opposite extreme of "apolitical" insulation from the political system.

NOTE: A coup may be coded for any combination of the six. All coups coded for "hierarchy" are also coded for "autonomy" but the converse does not hold.

Corporate Resources

Military coup-makers are apparently dissatisfied with the state of one or more of the following concerns:

Type A—pay, promotions, appointments, assignments, and/or retirements.

Type B—budget allocations, training facilities/arrangements, and/or interservice favoritism.

Type C—general military policy and/or the level and nature of support for military operations (e.g., war, insurgency, suppression, and the maintenance of order).

Type D—some combination of types A through C.

NOTE: A coup may be coded for only one of the four types.

NOT-SO-CORPORATE

Individual

Military coup-makers apparently perceive a threat to their personal position(s) and resource base(s) either within the military organization, the political system, or both.

Suborganizational Groups

Military coup-makers apparently perceive a threat to:

military faction—the position(s) and resource base(s) of a suborganizational clique to which they belong.

sectional group—the position(s) and resource base(s) of a primordial or ethnoregional group to which they belong.

both—the position(s) and resource base(s) of a suborganizational clique to which they belong. The clique or faction is based upon a common primordial or ethnoregional group membership.

NOTE: A coup may be coded for subcategory "Individual" and/or only one of the subcategories of "Suborganizational Groups."

Personnel Adjustments

Military coup-makers apparently are attempting:

reductionist—to reduce the size of a previously successful coup coalition or to anticipate or to counter the possibility of a reductionist effort.

preventive—to forestall a perceived extra-legal attempt to prolong the stay in office of a chief executive.

preservative—to assist an extra-legal attempt to prolong the stay in office of a chief executive.

restorative—to re-seat a chief executive deposed by a previous coup.

preemptive—to veto the coming to power (whether legally or illegally) of a specific individual or group (whether civilian or military).

NOTE: A coup may be coded for only one of the five types.

SOCIETAL "RESIDUAL"

Corporate and not-so-corporate grievances must be either absent or minimal. Military coup-makers apparently and primarily are attempting:

Strikingly Reformist—to correct societal injustices and abuses.

Order Maintenance—to suppress public disorder for the sake of maintaining public order.

NOTE: A coup may be coded for either "Strikingly Reformist" or "Order Maintenance" but not for both.

SUPPLEMENTARY DATA

Political Ideology

Military coup-makers apparently can be characterized as either more or less comfortable with the societal status quo (relative to the orientation apparently held by the coup's target). Coup-makers are decoded as:

More liberal, if less comfortable;

More conservative, if more comfortable;

Mixed, if both of the above apply;

Absent, if there is no difference; or

Ambiguous, if none of the above judgments can be made.

Party Alliances

Military coup-makers apparently are allied with either an opposition party or a wing of the ruling party. (The goals of the civilian allies are not necessarily those of the military coup-makers.)

Electoral Decisions

Military coup-makers apparently are attempting either to forestall an impending election (within one year) or to negate the results of an *immediately previous* election (within six months). Only the elections that involve a chief executive are considered.

NOTE: All coups are coded for each of the three categories. The three categories are considered as supplementary to the grievance categories and are discussed as appropriate.

APPENDIX B
MILITARY COUPS 1946-1970[a]

Algeria	6/31/62(S); 9/29/63(C); 6/30/64(U); 6/19/65(S); 12/14/67(U).
Argentina	9/18/51(U); 6/16/55(U); 9/16/55(S); 11/13/55(S); 6/9/56(U); 6/20/59(U); 6/13/60(U); 11/30/60(U); 8/11/61(U); 3/28/62(S); 8/8/62(C); 9/19/62(S); 12/11/62(U); 4/2/62(U); 6/27/66(S); 6/8/70(S).
Bolivia	6/13/46(U); 7/18/46(S); 8/27/49(U); 7/22/50(U); 5/16/51(S); 4/9/52(S); 1/6/53(U); 6/20/53(U); 11/9/53(U); 10/4/57(U); 5/14/58(U); 10/21/58(U); 6/26/59(U); 3/19/60(U); 11/3/64(S); 9/26/69(S); 10/4/70(U); 10/6/70(S).
Brazil	8/22/54(S); 11/11/55(S); 11/21/55(S); 2/11/56(U); 12/3/59(U); 8/25/61(C); 9/12/63(U); 3/30/64(S); 8/31/69(S).
Burma	9/26/58(S); 3/2/62(S).
Burundi	10/18/65(U); 7/8/66(S); 11/29/66(S).
Cambodia	3/18/70(S).
Cen. Afr. Rep.	12/31/65(S); 4/10/69(U).
Colombia	6/13/53(S); 5/10/57(S); 5/2/58(U); 10/11/61(U).
Congo (B)	8/15/63(S); 6/27/66(C); 8/2/68(C); 8/30/68(S); 3/22/70(U).
Costa Rica	4/2/49(U).
Cuba	3/10/52(S); 4/29/56(U); 9/5/57(U).
Dahomey	10/28/63(S); 11/29/65(S); 12/22/65(S); 12/17/67(S); 12/10/69(S).
Dom. Rep.	5/30/61(U); 7/?/61(U); 1/16/62(U); 1/18/62(S); 9/25/63(S); 4/24/65(C).
Ecuador	3/14/47(U); 8/23/47(S); 8/30/47(S); 11/9/47(U); 7/26/49(U); 7/15/50(U); 3/3/52(U); 12/23/54(U); 8/7/56(U); 11/7/61(C); 7/11/63(S); 3/29/66(S).
Egypt	7/23/52(S); 2/24/54(C).
El Salvador	12/14/48(S); 1/5/49(S); 10/26/60(S); 1/24/61(S).
Eq. Guinea	3/4/69(U).
Ethiopia	12/14/60(U).
France	5/13/58(C); 4/21/61(U).
Gabon	2/17/64(U).
Ghana	2/24/66(S); 4/17/67(U).
Greece	4/21/67(S); 12/13/67(U).
Guatemala	7/18/49(U); 3/29/53(U); 6/27/54(U); 6/29/54(S); 1/20/55(U); 10/24/57(S); 11/13/60(U); 11/25/62(U); 3/30/63(S).
Haiti	1/11/46(S); 5/10/50(S); 12/12/56(S); 4/2/57(S); 5/21/57(C); 4/24/70(U).

Honduras	8/1/56(U); 10/21/56(S); 2/7/59(U); 7/12/59(U); 9/8/61(U); 10/3/63(S).
Indonesia	10/11/56(U); 11/16/56(U); 12/22/56(U); 2/10/58(U); 3/11/66(S).
Iran	8/13/53(S).
Iraq	7/14/58(S); 3/7/59(U); 2/8/63(S); 7/3/63(U); 11/13/63(U); 11/18/63(S); 9/16/65(U); 6/29/66(U); 7/17/68(S); 7/30/68(S); 1/20/70(U).
Jordan	4/13/57(U).
Laos	12/31/59(C); 8/9/60(S); 9/10/60(S); 12/8/60(U); 4/19/64(C); 1/31/65(U); 3/28/65(U); 4/16/65(U); 10/21/66(U).
Lebanon	12/30/61(U).
Libya	9/1/69(S).
Mali	11/19/68(S).
Nepal	12/15/60(S).
Nicaragua	5/25/47(S).
Nigeria	1/14/66(C); 7/28/66(C); 5/30/67(U); 8/9/67(U).
Oman	7/23/70(S).
Pakistan	10/7/58(S); 10/27/58(S); 3/25/69(S).
Panama	11/19/49(S); 5/9/51(S); 9/?/62(U); 10/11/68(S); 12/14/69(U).
Paraguay	6/9/46(U); 3/7/47(U); 6/3/48(S); 10/25/48(U); 1/30/49(S); 2/26/49(U); 5/4/54(S); 12/21/55(U).
Peru	7/4/48(U); 10/3/48(U); 10/27/48(S); 6/14/50(U); 8/10/54(U); 2/16/56(U); 7/18/62(S); 3/3/63(S); 10/3/68(S).
Portugal	10/10/46(U); 4/10/47(U); 1/1/62(U).
Senegal	12/17/62(U).
Sierra Leone	3/21/67(U); 3/23/67(S); 4/17/68(S).
Somalia	12/10/61(U); 10/21/69(S).
S. Korea	10/19/48(U); 5/16/61(S).
S. Vietnam	11/10/60(U); 2/27/62(U); 11/1/63(S); 1/30/64(S); 9/13/64(U); 12/19/64(S); 1/27/65(S); 2/19/65(C); 6/12/65(S).
S. Yemen	3/20/68(U).
Sudan	11/17/58(S); 3/2/59(C); 5/22/59(U); 11/9/59(U); 10/26/64(S); 12/27/66(U); 5/24/69(S).
Syria	3/30/49(S); 8/14/49(S); 12/19/49(S); 11/29/51(S); 2/25/54(S); 9/28/61(S); 3/28/62(U); 3/30/62(C); 3/8/63(S); 7/18/63(U); 2/23/66(S); 9/7/66(U); 2/26/69(C); 11/13/70(S).
Thailand	11/8/47(S); 4/6/48(S); 9/22/48(U); 2/26/49(U); 6/29/51(U); 11/29/51(S); 9/16/57(S); 10/20/58(S).

APPENDIX B (Continued)

Togo	1/13/63(S); 1/12/67(S).
Turkey	5/27/60(S); 2/22/62(U); 5/20/63(U).
Uganda	2/22/66(S).
Upper Volta	1/3/66(S).
Venezuela	12/10/46(U); 7/26/47(U); 9/12/47(U); 11/24/48(S); 9/29/52(U); 11/30/52(S); 1/1/58(U); 1/22/58(S); 7/21/58(U); 9/7/58(U); 4/19/60(U); 9/12/60(U); 12/21/60(U); 2/20/61(U); 6/26/61(U); 5/4/62(U); 6/2/62(U); 10/30/66(U).
Yemen	2/17/48(U); 4/2/55(U); 9/26/62(S); 11/4/67(S); 8/23/68(C).
Zaire	9/14/60(S); 11/25/65(S); 7/5/67(U).

a. Coup outcomes: S=successful; U=unsuccessful; C=compromise. Coded data is available for all 274 coups, but sufficient grievance data are restricted primarily to an n of 229.

APPENDIX C
MILITARY COUP DATA SOURCES

World news digests
   Facts-on-File
   Keesing's Contemporary Archives

Regional news digests
   Africa Diary
   Africa Recorder
   Africa Report
   Africa Research Bulletin: Political, Social, and Cultural Series
   Arab Report and Record
   Hispanic World Report/Hispanic American Report

Newspapers
   The *Times* (London)
   The New York *Times*

Political histories and country/case studies

   Latin America
      Alexander (1958a, 1958b, 1964, 1970); Anderson (1970a, 1970b); Astiz (1969); Barager (1970); Beltran (1968); Blanksten (1951, 1970); Brill (1967); Calvert (1969); Dix (1967); Dulles (1970); Einaudi (1969); Fagg (1965); Ferms (1969); Fluharty (1957); Galbraith (1966); Gallo (1969); Goldrich (1970); Hennessy (1970); K. F. Johnson et al. (1969); Lieuwen (1964, 1965); Logan (1968); Lott (1970); Malloy (1970); Marrett (1969); Martz (1959, 1962); Moreno (1967, 1970); Needler (1964); Parker (1964); Patch (1959); A. Payne (1968); Pendle (1963); Peterson (1970); Pike (1967); Poppino (1966); Ross (1956); Rotberg (1971); Rowe (1964a); Schmitt and Burks (1963); Skidmore (1967); Springer (1968); Stokes (1959); Taylor (1968); Thomas (1971); Wiarda (1968a, 1968b, 1969).

Arab

Be'eri (1970); Bell (1970); Carleton (1950); Dann (1969); First (1970); Grundy (1968); Hadded (1971); Henderson (1965); Holt (1963); Hudson (1968); Humbraci (1966); Ingrams (1964); Khadduri (1952, 1963, 1969a, 1969b); Kilner (1959); Lenczowski (1965); Lewis (1966); O'Ballance (1971); Ottaway and Ottaway (1970); Patai (1958); Perlmutter (1969b); Quandt (1969); al-Sadat (1957); Schmidt (1968); Seale (1965); Shwadran (1960); Torrey (1963, 1964); Vatikiotis (1961, 1967, 1968, 1969); Wenner (1967, 1970); Zartman (1970); Ziadeh (1957).

S.E. and E. Asia

Buttinger (1967); Butwell (1963); "B. D." (1952); Dommen (1964); Donnison (1970); Duncanson (1968); Dupuy (1961); Fall (1969); Feith (1962); Feith and Lev (1963); Henderson (1968); Hindley (1968); Jumper and Normand (1964); Kahin and Lewis (1969); Kim (1968); Leifer (1970); Oh (1968); Riggs (1966); "S. H." (1949); Shaplen (1965, 1969); Silverstein (1964); Smith (1964); Sohn (1968); Trager (1962); Wilson (1962, 1964).

Sub-Saharan Africa

Bayne (1969); Clapham (1968); Dalby (1967); DuBois (1969); First (1970); Fisher (1969); Garin (1970); Greenfield (1965); Grundy (1968); Gutteridge (1969); Kirk-Greene (1971); Kraus (1966, 1969, 1970); Legvold (1970); Lefever (1970); Lemarchand (1967, 1968); Levine (1968); LeVine (1967, 1968); Lloyd (1967); Nelkin (1967); Niven (1967); Price (1971); Skurnik (1968, 1970); Willame (1970); Young (1965); Zolberg (1968, 1969).

South Asia

Avery (1965); Cottam (1964); Dupree (1969); Haddad (1965); Harris (1965); Joshi and Rose (1966); Ozbudun (1966); Sayeed (1967); Stephens (1963); Ulman and Tachau (1965); Weekes (1964); Weiker (1963); Wilcox (1965); Yalman (1968); Ziring (1971).

Europe

Campbell and Sherrard (1968); Kelly (1965); Lang (1968); Legg (1969); Meisel (1962); Menard (1967); Papandreou (1970).

APPENDIX D
AVERAGE NUMBER OF SOURCES UTILIZED PER COUP
FOR ACTUAL DATA-MAKING PURPOSES BY COUNTRY

	PH	WD	RD	NA
Latin America				
Argentina	2.25	1.06	0.75	0.25
Bolivia	0.78	1.11	0.50	1.17
Brazil	2.11	0.33	0.56	0.00
Colombia	2.25	0.00	1.00	0.00
Costa Rica	2.00	1.00	0.00	0.00
Cuba	2.00	1.33	0.33	0.33

APPENDIX D (Continued)

	PH	WD	RD	NA
Latin America (Continued)				
Domi. Rep.	2.00	1.00	0.33	0.17
Ecuador	0.67	0.83	0.42	1.42
El Salvador	1.75	1.25	0.75	0.50
Guatemala	1.22	0.67	0.67	0.67
Haiti	2.14	1.00	0.14	0.71
Honduras	2.00	0.67	0.83	0.83
Nicaragua	2.00	1.00	0.00	2.00
Panama	0.60	1.00	0.20	1.80
Paraguay	0.38	1.13	0.25	1.00
Peru	2.00	0.78	0.33	0.67
Venezuela	1.17	0.56	0.67	0.78
Arab				
Algeria	3.00	1.20	0.40	0.40
Egypt	4.00	0.00	0.00	0.00
Iraq	2.91	1.00	0.27	0.45
Jordan	5.00	0.00	0.00	0.00
Lebanon	3.00	1.00	0.00	0.00
Libya	0.00	1.00	3.00	1.00
Oman	0.00	1.00	1.00	1.00
S. Yemen	2.00	0.00	3.00	2.00
Sudan	3.43	0.71	0.29	0.29
Syria	3.71	1.57	0.21	0.50
Yemen	2.20	0.80	0.00	0.20
S.E. and E. Asia				
Burma	3.50	1.50	0.00	0.50
Cambodia	1.00	1.00	0.00	2.00
Indonesia	1.20	0.40	0.00	0.20
Laos	1.56	1.33	0.00	0.22
S. Korea	2.50	1.50	0.00	0.00
S. Vietnam	2.33	1.33	0.00	0.33
Thailand	2.50	1.13	0.00	0.75
Sub-Saharan Africa				
Burundi	1.00	1.00	0.67	0.00
Cen. Afr. Rep.	1.50	1.50	1.00	0.00
Congo (B)	0.40	1.00	0.80	0.80
Dahomey	1.60	1.20	1.00	0.40
Eq. Guinea	0.00	1.00	0.00	2.00
Ethiopia	3.00	1.00	0.00	0.00
Gabon	0.00	3.00	3.00	0.00
Ghana	5.00	1.00	2.50	0.00
Mali	1.00	1.00	2.00	0.00
Nigeria	3.25	1.00	1.25	0.25
Senegal	0.00	1.00	0.00	0.00
Sierra Leone	1.67	1.33	1.33	0.33
Somalia	0.50	0.50	1.00	0.00
Togo	0.50	2.00	1.00	0.50

APPENDIX D (Continued)

	PH	WD	RD	NA
Sub-Saharan Africa (Continued)				
Uganda	0.00	1.00	1.00	1.00
Upper Volta	5.00	1.00	0.00	0.00
Zaire	.167	1.33	1.33	0.33
Other				
France	3.50	1.50	0.00	0.00
Greece	2.50	1.00	0.00	0.00
Iran	3.00	1.00	0.00	0.00
Nepal	1.00	0.00	0.00	0.00
Pakistan	2.33	0.33	0.00	0.00
Portugal	0.00	1.67	0.33	1.00
Turkey	3.67	1.00	0.00	0.00

WHERE: PH = political histories and country/case studies
WD = world news digest
RD = regional news digest
NA = newspaper article

WILLIAM THOMPSON is Assistant Professor of Government, Florida State University. He was granted the Ph.D. from the University of Washington in 1972, and was NIMH Post-Doctoral Fellow at the University of Minnesota. While currently preparing several other works on military coups d'état, his present major research interest is an empirical study of great power summit meetings, from 1815 to 1972.

A Better Way of Getting New Information

Research, survey and policy studies that say what needs to be said—
no more, no less.

The Sage Papers Program

Eight regularly-issued original paperback series that bring, at an unusually
low cost, the timely writings and findings of the international scholarly
community. Since the material is updated on a continuing basis, each
series rapidly becomes a unique repository of vital information.

Authoritative, and frequently seminal, works that NEED to be available

- To scholars and practitioners
- In university and institutional libraries
- In departmental collections
- For classroom adoption

Sage Professional Papers

COMPARATIVE POLITICS SERIES
INTERNATIONAL STUDIES SERIES
ADMINISTRATIVE AND POLICY STUDIES SERIES
AMERICAN POLITICS SERIES
CONTEMPORARY POLITICAL SOCIOLOGY SERIES
POLITICAL ECONOMY SERIES

Sage Policy Papers

THE WASHINGTON PAPERS

Sage Research Papers

SAGE PUBLICATIONS
The Publishers of Professional Social Science
Beverly Hills • London

PROFESSIONAL PAPER **SUBSCRIPTION** INFORMATION APPEARS ELSEWHERE ON THIS CARD

PIC 374/5

PROFESSIONAL PAPER **SUBSCRIPTION** INFORMATION APPEARS ELSEWHERE ON THIS CARD

MAIL TO
SAGE Publications / P.O. Box 5024 / Beverly Hills, Calif. 90210

orders from the U.K., Europe, the Middle East and Africa
should be sent to 44 Hatton Garden, London EC1N 8ER